THE FIRST
48 HOURS

The First 48 Hours

Spiritual Caregivers as First Responders

Jennifer S. Cisney
and
Kevin L. Ellers

Abingdon Press
Nashville

THE FIRST 48 HOURS
SPIRITUAL CAREGIVERS AS FIRST RESPONDERS

This book is printed on acid-free paper.

Library of Congress Cataloging-in-Publication Data

Cisney, Jennifer S.
   The first 48 hours : spiritual caregivers as first responders / Jennifer S. Cisney and Kevin L.
Ellers.
      p. cm.
   Includes bibliographical references.
   ISBN 978-1-4267-0014-9 (pbk. : alk. paper)
   1. Counseling—Religious aspects. 2. Crisis management—Religious aspects. 3. Emergency
management—Psychological aspects. 4. Pastoral counseling. 5. First responders. I. Ellers,
Kevin L. II. Title. III. Title: First forty-eight hours.
   BF636.68.C57 2009
   253.5—dc22

                                                                                    2009016423

11 12 13 14 15 16 17 18—10 9 8 7 6 5 4 3 2
MANUFACTURED IN THE UNITED STATES OF AMERICA

Contents

And Who Is My Neighbor?

But he, wanting to justify himself, said to Jesus, "And who is
my neighbor?"—(Luke 10:29)

"And who is my neighbor?" This pointed question posed by an expert in the law in Luke 10:29 is the pinnacle of a conversation that begins with a question about what one must do to inherit eternal life. In response Jesus tells what we now call the parable of the good Samaritan. This parable aptly illustrates a number of key principles that demonstrate how we care for others in times of crisis—the subject of this book. While the research field of crisis response is still relatively new, having only come into prominence during the last three decades, the principles of caring for individuals in crisis dates back beyond biblical times. Through the centuries, the church has played a critical role in providing much of the frontline crisis response care. Let's look at this familiar parable in Luke 10:25-37 (NIV).

> On one occasion an expert in the law stood up to test Jesus. "Teacher," he asked, "what must I do to inherit eternal life?"
>
> "What is written in the Law?" he replied. "How do you read it?"
>
> He answered: " 'Love the Lord your God with all your heart and with all your soul and with all your strength and with all your mind'; and, 'Love your neighbor as yourself.' "
>
> "You have answered correctly," Jesus replied. "Do this and you will live."
>
> But he wanted to justify himself, so he asked Jesus, "And who is my neighbor?"
>
> In reply Jesus said: "A man was going down from Jerusalem to Jericho, when he fell into the hands of robbers. They stripped him

of his clothes, beat him and went away, leaving him half dead. A priest happened to be going down the same road, and when he saw the man, he passed by on the other side. So too, a Levite, when he came to the place and saw him, passed by on the other side. But a Samaritan, as he traveled, came where the man was; and when he saw him, he took pity on him. He went to him and bandaged his wounds, pouring on oil and wine. Then he put the man on his own donkey, took him to an inn and took care of him. The next day he took out two silver coins and gave them to the innkeeper. 'Look after him,' he said, 'and when I return, I will reimburse you for any extra expense you may have.'

"Which of these three do you think was a neighbor to the man who fell into the hands of robbers?"

The expert in the law replied, "The one who had mercy on him."

Jesus told him, "Go and do likewise."

The questions and issues raised by this parable are still asked today. Just whom should I help in a world that is full of hurting people? How much should I help? Is it really my responsibility? Which charitable organization should I contribute to this year?

Frequently we use this biblical passage to demonstrate that we are to care for all people, not just our families, friends, or even those in our churches—but the stranger, the disenfranchised, the victimized, and the lost. In this book, we begin with this parable to stress that the people of God, powered by the Holy Spirit, are an active force enabled to bring amazing change to a hurting world. Here in Luke, Jesus reminds us that there is a correlation between our love for God and our social responsibility to put our love in action for those around us. There is a call to care for those who are in crisis, those who have been traumatized physically, emotionally, and spiritually by violence or disaster.

Since September 11, 2001, our nation has continually faced devastating disasters and mass shootings in schools, universities, and public places such as shopping areas, all of which have historically been viewed as places of safety. Let's look at a few statistics. At least 90 percent of United States citizens will be exposed to a traumatic event during their lifetime (Breslau et al., 1998). Suicide rates typically increase as much as 63 percent in the first year after an earthquake, by 31 percent in the first two years after a hurricane, and by almost 14 percent four years after a flood (Krug et al., 1998).

Approximately one million persons each year become victims of violent crime while at work (Bachman, 1994). To comprehensively list all of the traumatic events over the past few years would be a daunting and depressing task.

Crisis Intervention from a Personal Perspective

This book is a direct result of our years of experience and extensive training on the frontlines of human suffering as crisis responders, pastoral caregivers, and mental health clinicians. However, what have most greatly influenced us are the painful experiences of our own lives that have greatly shaped our views of crisis response. Both of us have clinical degrees, extensive graduate and postgraduate education, leadership in national crisis response teams for large organizations, and extensive responsibility for direct crisis response care at the frontlines. However, we also write this book from the halls of suffering. Personal trauma and loss have tempered our theories and greatly reshaped how we see things. We both agree that it is really difficult to understand the cries of suffering until you have personally experienced some of life's adversities yourself.

Goal of This Book

As authors, it is our goal that this book will serve as a practical guide to help you serve others in times of crisis, trauma, and loss in the early aftermath of critical incidents. We hope that it will help you as a person of faith be a more active presence in our hurting world. For Jesus the requirement for eternal life is to " 'love the Lord your God with all your heart and with all your soul and with all your strength and with all your mind'; and, '[love] your neighbor as yourself.' . . . Do this and you will live" (Luke 10:27-28 NIV).

Who is your neighbor? For a first responder, it is anyone in need.

CHAPTER ONE

Crisis Response 101

The Basics

Readers who have had any training in crisis response, even a basic course, might find the information in this chapter very elementary. However, we realize there will be readers who have never had any formal training in crisis intervention or crisis response. For those individuals, it is critical to get some basic information that is generally covered in all introductory courses. So, for veterans, feel free to skip this chapter. But if you want to stay with us, a good review of the basics never hurt anyone.

Definition of a "Crisis"

It is evident that major crisis events in our country have escalated in recent decades, but so have the smaller incidents that affect individuals, families, and communities on a daily basis. In order to give you an appropriate introduction to the field, we need to offer some definitions and delineations that will help you understand the "language" of crisis response. We would like to define terms like *critical incident, crisis, crisis intervention,* and *psychological first aid.* You will hear all these terms during training and work as a crisis responder, and you should be aware of the distinctions and how each term is used.

A "critical incident" is the actual event that occurs. A critical incident can be any event that has potential to overwhelm the coping ability of individuals or groups exposed to the trauma. These can be large-scale events, such as terrorist attacks, hurricanes, floods, school shootings, and such. But a critical incident can also be any traumatic event—even those that directly affect only a small number of individuals. An automobile accident, a suicide, or a house fire are also critical incidents and can affect the individuals and families directly involved just as intensely as a hurricane or terrorist attack. The impact is what we define as a "crisis." A crisis is an acute psychological reaction to a critical incident or some distressing life circumstance. The critical incident (the event) is often confused with the crisis (a person's adverse reaction to the event). *As a crisis responder, it is critical that you tailor your response to the reaction to the event rather than to the event itself.* This is a very important distinction to make because if you respond to the event rather than the crisis, you may focus your attention on individuals who may not be having a crisis or who are only mildly affected while you bypass others who may be severely affected and in need of attention. If our work as crisis responders has taught us anything, it is that you cannot predict an individual's reaction to any traumatic event by evaluation of the event alone. An individual's reaction is a complicated combination of factors including the individual's personality, trauma history, support systems, life circumstances, and many other elements that come together to determine how any specific individual will be affected by a traumatic event.

An example of the importance of this distinction can be seen in the following story of a crisis response team. A group of college students were attending a school sporting event on a Saturday afternoon. Their team was losing badly at half time, so instead of staying for the remainder of the game, they decided to leave and go back to the off-campus apartment shared by two of the women in the group, Elizabeth and Abby. When the group of six students arrived at the apartment, they walked in on a young man who had broken into the apartment with the goal of robbery. Because he was unarmed when he was interrupted by the group, he picked up a large kitchen knife from the counter and grabbed Elizabeth, who was standing closest to him. Holding the knife to her throat, he threatened to kill her if he was not allowed to leave the apartment safely. As he backed slowly toward the door, he held the knife to Elizabeth's throat while continuing to threaten her friends that if they made one move toward him he would slit her throat. Once out the door he pushed Elizabeth down and fled the scene. A crisis response team was later dispatched to the school to do a group crisis intervention, called a defusing, with the group of students. As the crisis responders took the students through the steps of the intervention, Elizabeth seemed calm and relatively unaffected by the incident. In fact, many of her friends seemed more upset than she was. For one of the crisis responders, this was difficult to comprehend. She repeatedly questioned Elizabeth about how she was doing, focusing much of the group time and attention on Elizabeth. Elizabeth was a Christian and explained that from the moment the man grabbed her, she began to pray. She stated that God had given her peace in that first moment, and she just knew that the man would not hurt her. She continued to pray—but for the young man holding the knife. She sensed he was scared and in trouble, but that he would not hurt her. While many people might have been deeply affected by this incident, this young woman never felt that her life was truly threatened. The Holy Spirit gave her peace that prevented her from experiencing a level of fear that would be normal for such a situation. The crisis responder was convinced Elizabeth would have a delayed psychological crisis once she realized that her life had been in danger. While this type of delayed response can occur, that was not the case for Elizabeth. She was fine immediately following the event and would tell the same story months and years later. This critical incident never became a crisis for her.

However, her roommate, Abby, had a much different reaction to the event. While police and crisis responders focused on Elizabeth because she had had the most obviously traumatic experience, Abby was experiencing a psychological crisis significantly more intense than that of any of the other students. She was quiet and said little to responders during the group interventions. The crisis responders did not spend any one-on-one time with Abby, and she didn't ask for any time. While she seemed a bit anxious during the intervention, her symptoms would present in the days following the event. Over the following days and weeks, Abby was obviously agitated and displayed symptoms of traumatic stress including difficulty concentrating or focusing, inability to sleep, lack of appetite, and crying spells. All of these things can be normal responses to a traumatic event. However, a month later those symptoms had not subsided and had, in fact, gotten worse. It became clear that this incident had a tremendous impact on Abby. She was later referred to counseling. In the counseling, she revealed to her therapist that about nine months prior to the robbery incident, she had been the victim of rape at a party on campus. She had never received help or counseling and had not spoken to anyone about the rape. When she experienced the robbery, even though she was not the one facing the immediate physical threat, all the terror and fear she felt during her rape was triggered, and the posttraumatic stress was much more intense for her because it was combined with a delayed traumatic stress from the rape. Like many people who suffer most in the aftermath of a crisis, Abby had a prior trauma that she had not processed, and it made her reaction to the current stressful event much more severe. Because the crisis responders only looked at the event of Elizabeth having a knife held to her throat, they missed the crisis being experienced by Abby.

Posttraumatic Stress

Now that you understand that we define a "crisis" not by an event but by the response of an individual or a group of people to an event, it is critical that you also have a very basic understanding of what occurs in the human brain and body during crisis. This very natural process leads to a state called "posttraumatic stress," also referred to as "critical incident stress." Posttraumatic stress is, again, a natural and adaptive part of human functioning. God provided us with this type of "alarm system," which helps us survive life-threatening situations. In our everyday language, we often refer to this reaction as the "fight or flight" response. When faced with danger or a situation that our brain interprets as dangerous, our bodies undergo a number of physiological and chemical changes. These changes are designed to help us "flee" the danger or "fight off" the danger, thus the term "fight or flight" response. Our brain releases chemicals in our bodies like adrenaline and cortisol. These hormones have many effects in our body, all of which are designed to be helpful in short-term dangerous or life-threatening situations. Physically, these effects prepare our bodies for fighting or fleeing by increased blood pressure and heart rate, providing maximum oxygen levels in the blood. Increased blood is sent to the extremities (arms and legs) so we can run faster and, in some cases, have increased strength. Significant changes in brain function occur as well. The function of the frontal cortex area of the brain is decreased after trauma. This area of the brain is responsible for much of our cognitive processing, rational thought, decision-making, and the integration of emotional and cognitive functioning. The function of the amygdala, the emotional center of the brain, is increased following trauma. The amygdala serves as the brain's memory bank and houses all our emotions, including fear and anger. Following trauma, the normal balance between our frontal cortex and the amygdala is disrupted (Ellers, Rikli, and Wright, 2006).

> When the brain functions normally, the system functions well. However, traumatic events have the power to significantly change the brain's functioning. Trauma can cause a "wounding" to the bodily systems and may overwhelm the ordinary functioning modes. Trauma can create an altered state of functioning that can impair one's ability to perform essential tasks and frequently leads to psychological decomposition, or a "dumbing down" effect of cognitive impairment. The brain's design allows it to function as a holistic unit to create balance and appropriate levels of functioning. Traumatic events can overwhelm components and cause an interruption of functioning. Thus, trauma survivors may experience vivid graphic thoughts or images of the traumatic event with little or no emotion. The survivor may also experience intense emotions, but without the thoughts or actual memories and an impaired ability to cognitively process these emotions.

The intrusiveness of traumatic events can be so invasive that they may seem to temporarily take control of one's life. Survivors may find that they are washed back and forth between reliving the trauma, and being overwhelmed by floods of intense emotion, impulsive action, intrusive thoughts, involuntary physiological responses, and numbness and immobilization. The decrease in functioning of the frontal cortex creates a lessened ability to do basic left brain functions. Survivors may find a decreased ability to appropriately assess danger and distinguish between real and false threats. It may also limit people from putting into words what they feel. Thus, survivors may have an increased startle response and hypervigilance, falsely perceiving that there is danger (Ellers, Rikli, and Wright, 2006).

These symptoms, along with many others, are referred to as posttraumatic stress. Posttraumatic stress is a normal, healthy response to trauma and should not be pathologized. Instead, it is helpful to survivors if crisis responders normalize this set of symptoms, making it clear to the survivors that what they are experiencing is a "normal response to an abnormal event." This book will help you learn to identify the physical, emotional, psychological, behavioral, and spiritual symptoms that indicate that someone is experiencing posttraumatic stress.

It will be your responsibility as a crisis responder to identify common responses to a critical incident and to educate people on normal and abnormal responses. More about the responses to crises or "symptoms" will be discussed in the chapter on assessment and referral. The rest of this book is dedicated to helping those who are in the midst of experiencing this normal response to a very difficult and unusual experience or set of circumstances in their lives. The good news is that most of the people we respond to in times of crisis will recover fully from these very difficult times in their lives. Most will never need counseling and will not have long-lasting problems as a result of the traumatic events. Crisis intervention is about walking with people through this difficult time and facilitating their recovery through steps that will help them access their resilience and support their natural recovery processes.

But crisis intervention is also about recognizing individuals who may be having symptoms that go beyond normal posttraumatic stress or who seem at risk for further problems. The symptoms of posttraumatic stress are only normal and helpful within a limited time frame. For the majority of people who have experienced a traumatic event, posttraumatic stress symptoms will begin to subside within a few days. Within a few weeks, their brains and their bodies will be functioning normally again. However, for a small group of survivors, the symptoms not only persist, they can actually get worse. When the symptoms continue beyond one month or they are very severe, the individual needs to be assessed by a mental health professional. When normal posttraumatic stress does not resolve, it can become an anxiety disorder called Posttraumatic Stress Disorder or PTSD. All the steps we describe in this book are helpful for symptoms that are within the normal range. We want to make it clear that this book does not offer methods for treating

6

individuals with PTSD. But this book will help you, as a crisis responder, know when a person in crisis needs to be referred to a mental health professional. Again, most people will need only the care, compassion, and competence of a trained crisis responder. The next chapter discusses one of the most basic helping concepts: how and when to be present in the lives of those in times of crisis.

CHAPTER TWO
The Power of Presence

Will I Stop?

The hours dragged by as the family waited for any news of the elementary-age autistic boy who had been missing in a rural community. The child had been left in the care of his teenage sister and unbeknownst to her, he had slipped out of the home. Manny, a volunteer chaplain, had been working at the search and rescue scene. After a night of searching, the team found the missing boy dead in a nearby pond. Manny joined with another chaplain as they went to tell an anxious family that their son was dead. After he told the family, Manny, a stranger to the family, understood the importance of linking the family with a local support system. Manny asked if they were a part of a church congregation. The family gave him the name of their local pastor whom Manny then called. Manny told the pastor what had happened and said that the family gave his name as their pastor. The pastor said that he was fairly new to the congregation and he didn't know the family. Manny stressed the urgency of the situation and the emotional state of the family and then told him again that the family said he was their pastor and that they attended his church, and that they *really* needed him to come be with them. The pastor responded, "I don't know them, and I am not coming." Shocked, Manny had a sinking feeling in the pit of his stomach as he hung up. What was he going to tell the family? What message did this give to the many volunteers who had searched tirelessly, giving their time to help a family they did not know who was in need? What did this say about the church more generally?

In the account of the good Samaritan, a priest and a Levite both pass by the man before the Samaritan stopped to help. While many have written about why they did not stop, the real question for us is, *Who will stop in the face of human suffering to give their time and resources to someone who is in need?* Often there is no reward, no acknowledgment, no media present to view this good deed. So why should we stop? And what would make us stop? Before we judge this local pastor too harshly, perhaps we should stop to do a self-assessment. If you are like us, there have been many times in the course of our ministry when we have passed by on the other side of the road. Why do we fail to stop? What are the barriers to reaching out to hurting individuals?

Why Don't We Stop? Common Barriers to Stopping

The Day the Traffic Did Not Stop in Hartford

On June 8, 2008, *The New York Times* ran an article with the headline "The day the traffic did not stop in Hartford" (Applebome, 2008). The article opened with the words, "The video of a 78-year old man being tossed in the air after being hit by a car and then left in the street like a discarded food wrapper would have been hideous whoever the victim." This shocking video footage, which was captured by a police traffic camera, was broadcast by the news networks, and six months later was still playing on *YouTube,* graphically shows the victim as he is flipped upside down through the air to lie motionless on the street. While the image of the man being hit by the car is shocking, what is far more disturbing is the footage of the man lying on the street alone with none of the bystanders rushing to his side. The accident was witnessed by several people on the sidewalk and the occupants of at least three vehicles. The drivers of all three vehicles present at the time of the accident fled the scene without stopping, and none of the bystanders who witnessed the accident stepped to the man's aid. It is unbelievable to watch the video as nine vehicles pass him without stopping. People walk by or stop and look, but no one seems to do anything to stop traffic or comfort him until a police cruiser on its way to another call happens to drive upon the scene.

Who was this man? It probably seemed like a normal day to Angel Arce Torres, known as Ponce, as he bought milk at the corner store and walked across the street. He surely had no idea that within minutes his world would literally be flipped upside down, and, while he would live, he would be paralyzed.

Like the victim in the parable of the good Samaritan, adversity often hits us with little or no warning. But when it strikes, we desperately need others. What is it that compels us to stop what we are doing to help another person in distress, and what are some of the barriers that keep us from stopping to help? As I watched the video, I felt a rising sense of anger and helplessness as the man lay motionless on the street alone for what seemed like eternity. Have you ever needed help from a stranger?

Perhaps the observers of Ponce's accident understood that it could be dangerous to move him and had no idea of how to help. However, the power of simply being present would have been a comfort to him and his family. One of the things we hear from survivors who have lost a loved one suddenly or unexpectedly is that they did not want their loved one to die alone. What often haunts family members of murder victims is that the last person that their loved one saw was the one who intended to do them harm.

It is irrelevant whether the man in the video was an upstanding citizen or a homeless person; he still needed a compassionate presence. An interview with Ponce's son validates this fact. According to *The New York Times* article:

> "But, of course, that man lying on Park Street might have been a homeless person or a drug user, and he might be Ponce with a container of milk, but he was still a human being," said Mr. Torres' son, Angel Arce. "If we can't all be heroes, any human being, in the most traumatic moment of his life, deserves someone to stop traffic, someone to hold his hand until help arrives, deserves someone who would have responded the way that Ponce almost certainly would have." Ponce's son goes on to say, "It makes me angry and it leaves me hurt, to think of him there and no one to grab his hand, to offer comfort. He was always there helping everyone in their time of need, and in his time, no one was there for him." (Applebome, 2008)

Fear of Personal Risks as a Barrier

Helping others may involve certain risk to you personally. Those who worked in the aftermath of the 9/11 attacks on the World Trade Center faced many hazards as they worked under adverse conditions and breathed in toxins and dust particles that may still have a long-term impact on their health. One volunteer who helped in New Orleans after Hurricane Katrina had a history of lung problems. After he returned from working long hours in New Orleans, he died of a lung infection that was likely exacerbated by the disaster. Sometimes there are personal and professional risks that we may have to take to help others. It is a risk that we must carefully weigh, because becoming a casualty yourself helps no one.

When I (Kevin) was serving on a church staff just after seminary, a caring and compassionate friend stopped on her way home from church on an icy road at the bottom of a hill to assist a man in a car that had slid off the road. Jane was driving a four-wheel-drive vehicle and thought she could help. However, she did not stop to consider the risks—for example, that others coming down the hill would also not be able to stop. She was hit by another vehicle, and the teenage boy she was taking home witnessed the traumatic event. Not only did Jane die shortly after the accident, but the boy suffered long-term psychological and emotional consequences.

Taking care of ourselves is critical as we take care of others. Churches with crisis response teams must carefully assess the critical incidents to protect the team members and safeguard their physical, emotional, and spiritual exposure while also providing an opportunity to process their experiences.

Compassion Fatigue and Burnout as a Barrier

We must look not only at the physical risks but at the emotional risks as well. Working with hurting and grieving individuals is messy. You have to get in the trenches with them; and if you are a compassionate caregiver, you can't help getting dirty as well. The cumulative impact of caring for hurting people can take a toll. A common sign of burnout is just not caring. One day an extremely compassionate caregiver called his supervisor while serving in a disaster zone. He had been working for months providing emotional and spiritual care in the aftermath of a disaster. "I am worried and a little scared because something happened to me today that I have never experienced." He went on to say that he had been sitting with a person who was pouring his heart out after losing everything. The volunteer said, "I was sitting there listening to him and thinking 'I just don't care.'" This was atypical for this volunteer, who had given up both time and money in dedication to helping others. Unlike God, we as human beings are finite and we have a limited capacity to absorb the pain and problems of others. If we don't stop to wring out our emotional sponge or if we get overly absorbed caring for others without caring for our own needs, we are at great risk of becoming less compassionate and effective as caregivers.

There are two critical things that effective and balanced caregivers do to sustain themselves for the long haul. Effective caregivers set good boundaries and understand their limitations. I frequently tell zealous volunteers who are not practicing self-care that there is a need for only one Messiah and he already came. Sometimes we can get in a situation where we feel that we are the only one who can help another person. If this thought occurs to you, use it as a signal that you need to fortify your boundaries. Effective caregivers are astute in having an outlet to process and dump their emotional baggage from helping others, as well as having a well-established way of refueling emotionally, physically, relationally, and spiritually.

It was another busy travel day for me (Kevin) one late fall evening. I had been traveling nonstop for the past few weeks and had spent many months over the course of the year trying to help survivors of Hurricane Katrina put their lives back together in the aftermath of this huge storm. I was traveling to Canada to teach an intensive four-day training, and I was tired. I remembered the days when I used to preach a thirty-minute sermon twice a week and felt worn out at the end of the day. While that seemed easy now, teaching all day for multiple days was emotionally and physically draining, and I had been doing this nonstop for months. I was tired of traveling; I was tired of needy people with problems; I was tired of everything and everyone. I needed to conserve every last ounce of energy to get through the next four days. I pulled my newly purchased best friend and barrier to the world from my briefcase, a very noticeable set of noise-canceling headphones that allowed me to shut out the world and create a private space while still in a public place. I had previously purchased a great set of small noise-canceling headphones that had technically worked great. However, there was one problem: people often didn't see them and would talk to me anyway. No one could miss these puppies. As I connected them to my MP3 player with my relaxing inspirational music cued to play, my seatmate arrived before I could get them on my head. "Hi," he said. It would be totally rude not to respond. "Hi," I said without much enthusiasm. "Where you from?" he asked. I hesitated; this was going in the wrong direction. I looked longingly at my headphones as I busied myself with pretending to find something in my backpack. "Chicago," I finally muttered, trying to look as busy and uninterested as possible. *What's it going to hurt? Be nice; ask him in return where he is from.* The "be polite" voice of my mother echoed inside me, from one of those mom tapes that scolded me from deep within, activated no doubt by her assistant, the Holy Spirit. I found myself saying, "Where you from?" Okay, that just slipped out, but this would be it. Formalities over, he is probably from Chicago and I can go to sleep. But no. Guess where he was from? New Orleans. Guess what happened to him? He had lost everything.

It seemed like an eternity that I stared at my headphones. Suddenly a passage came vividly to mind. In Mark 6:30-34, Jesus was trying to spend time with his disciples, but the crowd was all around them, and they had been so busy that they hadn't even had time to eat. Jesus takes his disciples in a boat to go to a "solitary place" to get away from the crowd. However, the Bible records, "But many who saw them leaving recognized them and ran on foot from all the towns and got there ahead of them. When Jesus landed and saw a large crowd, he had compassion on them, because they were like sheep without a shepherd. So he began teaching them many things" (NIV). Convicted, I put my headphones down and ministered with the guy as he told his story. The headphones were for later.

Lack of Confidence as a Barrier

I (Kevin) was coordinating emotional and spiritual care teams to minister to workers and survivors in the Hurricane Katrina disaster operations. My team leader called me one day. "I'm having a problem with those new pastors you just sent down," he said. "What problem?" I asked. I was so tired of problems. "Well, they won't get out of the van," he said. "What do you mean they won't get out of the van?" I asked, trying to figure out what he was talking about. I struggled to keep my impatience from showing in my voice. I had instant visions of a sit-in taking place in a reenactment in the 1960s South by the Northern do-gooder invaders. He said, "The team will pull up to a neighborhood, and everyone gets out and goes to visit the people but them. They just sit in the van and talk. I'm not sure what to do." This is one of the frequent problems I find with people not used to doing outreach, especially when it is in an unfamiliar environment. I have always been amazed at how trained and experienced professionals are rendered incapable in situations when they are out of their comfort zone. I told the team leader that they were probably just not feeling comfortable yet, since they had just arrived, and to let them go through the day and see how they did. I asked him to break them up the next day and send them out with someone who had been getting out of the van and see how they did. After spending time with another person who had been working on the scene, they did fine.

Jesus strategically sent his disciples out in pairs (Mark 6:7, Luke 10:1). Teaming up with another person can be good for many reasons. When co-ministering with another person, you can draw on the strength of the other, who often sees things that you may miss. Each person brings a unique style; and if you are paired up with someone who complements your ministry style, you can make up for the other's weaknesses. Jim and Pam work very well together as a couple. He has a strong capacity to step back from the situation and objectively assess and clearly see the situation. Pam tends to get much more emotionally involved and quickly connects and engages deeply with those she ministers with. On the other hand, Jim can sometimes find it hard to build rapport and emotionally connect in the early stage of a helping relationship. However, Pam can easily find herself becoming too emotionally enmeshed in the helping relationship and may lose some objectivity, which Jim can help her balance. God designed us to be in relationship with others; and when we work as a team, the body of Christ is much stronger and far more effective.

Even trained and experienced helpers can feel inadequate to respond. I vividly remember the events of 9/11 and feeling overwhelmed by the magnitude of this event and my capacity to respond appropriately in the face of such tragedy. I pray that as crisis responders we never get to the place that we feel fully adequate to minister to the needs of people in immense suffering. It is our understanding of our inadequacy, regardless of how experienced, trained, and proficient we are that keeps us reliant on the wisdom and strengthening of the Holy Spirit.

Often we fail to stop to help others because of a misperception of what it is that we are supposed to provide. The following things are *not* what a ministry of presence is about in the immediate aftermath of trauma and loss:

- Having all the answers to the "why" questions
- Giving lots of advice
- Explaining the theological concepts
- Correcting what appears to be faulty theology in times of crisis
- Judging

Busyness as a Barrier

If you are like us, there never seems to be enough of you to go around. Pastors and church leaders alike are often pressed to make important decisions about their time, and the number of needy people seems to be endless. One of the important elements of this book is to encourage churches to seek ways to prepare laypeople to help care for the needs of the flock. Churches that depend primarily on the pastoral staff to meet the emotional and spiritual needs of the congregation will find it difficult to sustain growth and reach out to a hurting world. Unless the church truly functions as the body of believers to collectively care for the hurting, it will rarely grow. The larger body of believers need to actively exercise their spiritual gifts if they are going to stay healthy and grow emotionally and spiritually.

I (Kevin) love to work out at the gym. However, with my frequent travel schedule, sometimes I find that my routine gets interrupted for extended periods of time. Once out of my routine, I neglect to exercise and stretch my muscles. As my muscles stop growing, I become stiffer and less flexible, and it is harder to get started again. Spiritually mature people understand that they can't just take in spiritual calories without exercising their spiritual gifts. Spiritual obesity is as unhealthy as physical obesity.

However, sometimes the problem is not that we are inactive and don't want to or are fearful to help but rather that we don't stop to help because we are already helping someone who is even more needy. If an ambulance is rushing to the emergency room with a critically ill patient inside, the EMTs are not going to stop to help the stranded elderly motorist. They are taking care of someone who urgently needs their immediate care, and they are equipped to provide critical care to their patient. It does not mean, however, that they can't call roadside assistance to help the stranded motorist with her flat tire.

A common theme among thoughtful caregivers is that they feel guilt for not being able to do more. The very nature of being a follower of Christ compels us to take action for those who are hurting; and yet we have to, at the same time, balance our ministry to others with caring for ourselves, our spouses, and our children. Often it is the ones we love the most who suffer and get the least amount of our time or attention. If you are on the way to the daddy and daughter event at your school, do you stop and risk missing the event to deal with someone else's crisis, or do you call them back later or refer them to someone else? There are many people who can stop to help the stranded motorist, but there is no one else who can be Daddy at the daddy/daughter school event, and this is okay. There is a common misperception in some churches that the pastor must be available to anyone at any time regardless of circumstances.

It is critical that churches spread out the congregational care responsibility to protect the pastoral leadership while at the same time creating a system of care in which hurting people get the care they need. As Christians, we are all called to minister to the hurting; however, this perception varies broadly within faith communities. In some churches some congregants do not feel that they have received care unless it is from the senior pastor. If you pastor a church of twenty-five people, this may be a possibility. If, on the other hand, you are creating a vibrant and growing body of believers, this is impossible. In addition to the pastoral staff, there are many people within the body of believers who can be trained to be present and provide critical emotional and spiritual care to the hurting.

Measuring Personal Gain as a Barrier

Organizations like The Salvation Army respond to crises within their communities daily. However, those who organize these volunteer teams often complain that many of their volunteers only want to go to the "high-profile" disasters, not the local events. Why? Are not big events also made up of individual hurting beings? Is it another response to add to your vitae, another pin to put on your wall? Too often people want to serve only when they are emotionally compelled to do so. It is critical for caregivers to carefully assess their motivation to provide care. Do you want to serve on a disaster relief mission because your friends want you to go and it will be exciting? Or do you serve because there are hurting people who need the arms of the church around them? When you seek to help people in need, you will find hurting people long after the initial event has happened. When you seek to serve, not accomplish, this makes a huge difference in the way you approach whom and when you are going to help.

What Is at the Core of a Ministry of Presence?

Once we realize what survivors really need, it takes away a lot of the pressure that we put on ourselves to perform. What does it mean to really be present with someone? Jennifer and I define a ministry of presence as being *fully with another person, exhibiting a non-anxious, comfortable presence while demonstrating "God with us" through the interconnectedness of the human interaction. When people are in crisis and hurting, they usually crave the safe, comforting presence of others.*
An effective ministry of presence provides

- A comforting and non-anxious presence
- An environment of safety
- Being emotionally and spiritually present in the moment
- Demonstrating "I will be with you"
- Good listening

- Being other-focused not self-focused
- Acceptance and a lack of judgment
- Being a servant and meeting basic needs
- Good thinking skills to help survivors sort through the tasks at hand

When we review the above list, it may not seem that the concepts should be all that difficult. However, from working in the crisis field for many years and hearing the stories of survivors and those who helped and those who hurt, it is clear to us that these basic helping concepts are not always accomplished, even by well-meaning caregivers.

Simply put, a ministry of presence is primarily about *being* rather than *doing*. However, in saying this, an astute observer of the behaviors involved in an effective ministry of presence would observe simple acts of doing. In comparing the actions of effective and uneffective caregivers, it has become very clear to us that it is more about the *way* in which good caregivers do what they do. A ministry of presence is about the "art of being." In examining the life of Jesus, we see that he was masterful in the art of being. He clearly knew who he was and what he was about. He moved with purposefulness when faced with adversity and crisis situations. Note how he calmly dealt with, for example, the woman caught in adultery in John 8:4.

There was something about the person of Jesus that we would do well to strive to emulate. You may argue that he was fully divine and fully human, and thus we can never achieve this. True, but we are called to be Christ's followers and to emulate his actions and behaviors although we are marred and distorted (1 Cor. 13:12). The Gospels record numerous instances in which we find Jesus' disciples full of doubt and worry; and yet, Jesus through his presence brings calm to the situation. Although he often takes action, there is something about his presence that brings great relief and peace.

When I (Kevin) watched the video clip of Ponce (mentioned above) being hit, I vicariously experienced a heightened level of anxiety because my accident closely paralleled his, except in my case many people did stop to help. I distinctly remember a woman who stopped her car and rushed to my side. She did nothing but tell me that the ambulance was coming and hold my hand. I will never forget how comforting her compassionate kindness was even though I was in pain and feeling anxious about what would happen to me. I will never forget the feeling that I had when I woke up after surgery to see my parents sitting by the bedside. They had driven most of the night to be there. I have no idea of what they said or did. I just remember hearing my mom saying, "Oh, sweetie," and seeing my parents' smiles, feeling their loving touch, and listening to their prayers for me. It brought me substantial comfort.

As Jesus was about to leave this earth, he told his frightened and anxious followers that he was not going to leave them alone. He told them about the Holy Spirit, the Comforter, the one who comes alongside us. In Matthew 28:18-20 Jesus returns to visit his disciples after the resurrection. Struggling with direction, full of doubt and fear, they believe they are alone. It is then that Jesus directs them to their ongoing mission, and he promises them that they are not alone. He comforts his disciples with his words, "And surely I am with you always, to the very end of the age" (28:20 NIV).

God promises that we are not alone. When you show up on a scene where a person is in trauma or crisis, you visibly demonstrate God's presence in a tangible way. You become symbolic of the hands, the feet, the arms of Christ. These are arms that can be immediately felt and that bring comfort, healing, and grace in times of need.

In my work as a chaplain for many years, it has always been interesting to see the dynamic in the room change when the person's pastor, group leader, close friend, or family shows up. There can be an almost visible release of tension that occurs that is readily noticeable to the outsider. It says, "Here I am, I will be with you. We will figure it out together."

When Presence Isn't Ministry

People often fail to understand the power that one's presence can bring to hurting people. While completing my (Kevin's) clinical pastoral education (CPE) units in the hospital setting, the group of which I was a part had many discussions relating to the ministry of presence. It was often difficult to define what was "happening" when "nothing was happening." When working with trauma survivors, I often ask them what was most helpful to them in the midst of their pain. Often they indicate how someone came to be with them. When we are hurting and in crisis, we often want someone to be there, and yet we all know people who have tried to help us but we didn't find their presence helpful or comforting. When I teach about the ministry of presence, I often ask the class, "Is ministry always presence and is presence always ministry?" It is important to understand that your physical presence does not necessarily mean that you are truly present with someone and that there are different dimensions of presence.

Physically Present but Emotionally Absent

You can be physically present but not emotionally present. I used to know a pastor who could sit with you only for about five minutes before he would start looking at his watch or out the window. Although he would physically stay longer than those five minutes with people, he emotionally tuned out. You could watch people begin to shut down as he emotionally disconnected.

When You Aren't Wanted

Your presence is not ministry if you are not wanted there. Sometimes people don't know you or may want to be alone. It is critical that caregivers become astute in reading the nonverbal cues that people give. It may have nothing to do with you; they may just want to be alone. Sometimes survivors are so overwhelmed by the numbers of people coming and going that they have limited capacity to connect with others. Understand that though you may not be needed at a given time, it does not mean that you won't be needed later. As a chaplain, your initial introduction to survivors may not be warmly received. However, often in stopping back later to check in, you may find them much more receptive. Too often, however, when caregivers feel rejection, they are reluctant to return, even though that may be when they are needed the most.

Physically Absent but Emotionally Present

Because of my (Kevin's) intensive travel schedule, many of my closest friends are scattered around the country. Often when I am in my deepest pain, I have not been able to have my closest friends physically present with me, and yet they have a great capacity to be there emotionally and spiritually. You can be present through the power of prayer. Many times, when I have been going through a difficult time, I could feel the power of the prayers of others in my life. A thoughtfully written card or e-mail can say "Hey—I love you and haven't forgotten you." I will never forget a particularly low point in my life. I was lying on the floor of the house in incredible pain after the car accident. It seemed that all my hopes and dreams had been ripped away. I was feeling isolated and sorry for myself, and life didn't seem worth living anymore. The phone rang and it was my boss. I had been off work for a while, and she just called to say that God had been directing her to pray for me, and she wanted me to know that many people were praying for me; they loved me and were concerned about me and missed me. We talked for a while, and I could feel the power of her presence and all the others who were praying for me as she mediated this powerful presence to me even though she was physically many miles away.

How Can the Church Be Present for People?

The church, probably more than any other organized group of individuals, has endless opportunities to be present in the lives of people. The biblical model of the New Testament church is not a building, program, or institution. The "church" is simply people who are designed to be in relationships in which they lovingly and intentionally give of themselves to others and God. God is a relational being who designed us to be relational beings as well. How is it that we selflessly give ourselves to others so that we can intentionally live within interconnected relationships?

Too often we are more concerned about programs than relationships. However, I am firmly convinced that people are healed not through programs or enhanced theological understanding but rather through relationship. God has chosen the church to be the visible expression of his love for us and our love for others. To show up in the lives of hurting people, not with a message of "I will fix you," but rather, "I will be with you" is a powerful fulfillment of God's intent for the church. If we truly understand that all we really have to do is to love people and be with them and allow the Holy Spirit to do his job with them, it takes a lot of pressure off of us to perform. We need to empower our congregations to understand that their number one task is to love people and to be the present, visible sign of God's love for them in the midst of their struggles.

The Psalms speak many messages to us about the portraits of a suffering humanity. There can be few things more disheartening than experiencing the silence of God in the midst of despair. The lament of Psalm 77 launches straight into the cries of the psalmist. In reading the psalm, it becomes quickly evident that the greatest issue for the psalmist is not the nature of the precipitating incident but rather the psalmist's perception of God's silence, failure to show up, and the rejection in the midst of his distress. It is against the backdrop of the larger drama of a crisis of faith that the immediate incident is contextualized.

Verses 1-2 indicate that there have been many prayers that have not been answered. The psalmist cries out not only by voice but also in the anguish of the soul. "My soul refused to be comforted," (v. 2 NIV) drives him to reach out with his body: "I stretched out untiring hands" (v. 2 NIV). This is not an individual who offers a placid prayer for an improvment in the inconvenient circumstances of life; this is someone who, from the anguish of the soul, pleads with God late into the dark recesses of the night for divine intervention.

The perspective, characters, and the roles are also different as God is portrayed not as redeemer or shepherd of his people but instead as the God of the skies at whom the earth quakes. Interestingly, despite this awesome and dramatic display of power, verses 19 and 20 state this about God: "Your path led through the sea, / your way through the mighty waters, / though your footprints were not seen. / You led your people like a flock / by the hand of Moses and Aaron." This serves as a reminder that even in the mighty revelations of God's power, his acts can only be recognized by faith. God's presence and guidance are often accomplished through the lives of those he calls to service like Moses and Aaron (v. 20 NIV).

This psalm openly addresses a cry to God despite the psalmist's feeling God's absence and rejection. The psalmist does not attempt to mask the despair, abandonment, and rejection beneath a religious facade. There is an honest openness about his failure to reach God and about his past attempts to find consolation that had fallen empty. The psalm progresses from the cries of lament for deliverance to an appeal to the very character and acts of God with songs of praise. When hope is gone and feelings are not there, the psalmist chooses to remember and place his trust in the One who, though not seen, continued to lead his people like a flock by the hand of Moses and Aaron. We must understand that it is the church that God chooses to use to comfort and guide people through the dark chaos of the painful circumstances that life throws at them. And like Moses and Aaron, we are God's choice to demonstrate his presence in the lives of people in pain. There is no plan B.

Angels Unaware

In Hebrews 13:1-2 we are exhorted to "keep on loving each other as brothers. Do not forget to entertain strangers, for by so doing some people have entertained angels without knowing it" (NIV). There are more than 300 references to angels within the Bible. In recent years there has been a renewed fascination with angels. This is not new; the early church even had to directly address the angel worship that was occurring. There are shops dedicated to selling angel-related goods—from bumper stickers to desk sculptures. Most of these angels have glistening wings and are dressed in beautiful, white, flowing robes. However, there is another important portrayal of angels in Scripture in which these beings look very different. In fact, the more common biblical portrayal of angels closely mirrors the actions and look of common beings. Often those who encountered these angels did not know until later that they had been in the presence of an angel.

Many of us have watched the Christmas classic *It's a Wonderful Life*, in which the angel Clarence interacts with George Bailey. As adults, childhood fantasy lives with us. There is something about angels that represents magic and mystery. We want angels to look special—heavenly, perhaps. Too often this fantasy can stand in the way of our experiencing God's reality.

This is great good news to us because if we are honest, we relate much more to others in the trenches as personified Clarences, because we are all very far from being holy majestic beings! Seek to learn the art of being present with people in times of difficulty, and God can use this both for his glory and to make a long-lasting and immeasurable difference in the lives of those you touch. You may be someone's angel!

Quick Reference Tips for Providing a Ministry of Presence during the First 48 Hours

- Remember that it is possible to be present physically but not emotionally and spiritually present with survivors. Be on guard against getting distracted.
- Understand that being fully present with people in times of crisis is the first step in ministering to deeper needs.
- Sometimes just being there is more powerful than anything else you can do.
- Remember that when you are present, you represent God.
- Carefully watch a survivor's nonverbal language and know when it is time to go.
- Make sure that survivors have others who can be present with them throughout the duration.

Think about This

1. When have you struggled to come alongside someone in times of crisis and sorrow?

2. What are some of the barriers that keep people from reaching out to others in pain?

3. Describe a time in which someone provided a ministry of presence to you. What did it look like and what made it ministry?

4. Who do you know right now who may need a ministry of presence?

CHAPTER THREE
Safety in Times of Crisis

When my (Kevin's) girls were little, on cold days when we got the warm towels out of the dryer we would snuggle under them, and the girls would giggle at the warmth and the clean smell. I still feel nostalgic when I take out the warm towels today. For many years I worked in the emergency room as a chaplain with people in crisis. There were always warm blankets available that we would give to patients. It seemed like a hospitable (no pun intended) thing to do, because the emergency room was always cold. It also didn't help that the staff stripped the patients of their street clothes and bestowed on them the great honor of wearing an all-too-thin hospital gown that was sure to expose some part of the anatomy. I understood the practical side of this and would work with the staff to pass out the blankets to people when they were cold.

I understood the purpose of warm blankets from a whole new dimension, however, after my accident. It is something that I have heard from many other trauma survivors. I remember lying there on the bed waiting for tests and feeling all alone and completely vulnerable. As one of the nurses came in to check on me, she must have seen the tears in my eyes that I was so desperately trying to hide. She said, "You look cold," and brought me one of the warm blankets. It was similar to what my mom would have done when I was young. The nurse tucked the blanket in around me in a way that cocooned me in the bed. Then she stepped back and smiled. Not only did I feel the warmth of the blanket, but I distinctly remember feeling safe and cared for. Something about that simple act made a measurable difference for me, because it met a deep psychological, emotional, and, probably even, relational need. I have never forgotten the power of that interaction and how it helped me feel more secure in the midst of my crisis.

World-famous psychologist Abraham Maslow describes a "hierarchy of needs" that all human beings follow. The basic concept is that human beings, while capable of higher thought and spiritual growth and development, are only capable of focusing their energies on those "higher" levels of development or "self actualization" when the basic needs are met. Maslow's pyramid describing the hierarchy of human needs has, at its base, physiological needs. These are the elements that all humans need to stay alive, such as oxygen, food, water, and sleep. Once those physiological needs are met, the next level is composed of "safety needs."

Being Safe versus Feeling Safe

Being Safe

One of the most basic human needs is for safety, for ourselves and those we love. One component of a crisis is when someone perceives that their safety or the safety of others is threatened. The first step is to ensure that they truly are out of harm's way. We must confirm that the threat (real or perceived) that created the psychological crisis for them is over and there is no true threat to their physical safety. In many cases, this is a given. However, there are situations where crisis responders will face the immediate need to provide individuals with physical safety. No emotional or spiritual care will be effective if the person is still in danger.

Crisis interveners need to help protect survivors. In the early aftermath of a critical incident, survivors may be at great risk of being injured again. Sometimes this risk comes from well-meaning people who try to help but actually do more harm by their words and actions. Sometimes they are hurt by people who have an agenda and perhaps even prey on survivors. These may be aggressive and insensitive members of the news media trying to get a story; they may be lawyers trying to get a case. We have seen lawyers arrive on the scene of a critical incident to solicit business. Unfortunately, those who harm may include well-intentioned but insensitive people who are inappropriately trying to evangelize in the time of crisis. People in the aftermath of trauma and loss are vulnerable, and we need to protect them as their normal coping and defense mechanisms are likely to be significantly impaired.

Survivors have to be protected not only from others but sometimes from themselves as well. Sometimes survivors can feel so overwhelmed by the event that they feel life is not worth living and even become suicidal. They may neglect to take care of themselves by not eating or drinking. Parents may be so distraught by the events that they neglect to take care of even the most basic needs of their children. Self harm is a very real danger for individuals following a significant trauma or loss. A primary mistake crisis responders can make is to underestimate this threat. Even otherwise emotionally stable and psychologically healthy individuals can experience a brief period of suicidal ideation or even homicidal thoughts when dealt a significant psychological blow. Remember that the brain often does not function normally in the immediate aftermath of trauma.

The prefrontal cortex of the brain is the area that helps us make decisions about right and wrong and helps us understand the consequences of our actions. This section of the brain acts as our filter to keep us from acting on impulses that may have negative consequences. And this is the part of our brain that is not as active in individuals who are in the throes of trauma. The rational portion of our brains that normally overrides destructive impulses is not in control during the first 48 hours following a traumatic event. Instead, the amygdala, the portion of our brain that is responsible for emotions such as fear and anger, is running the show. There may be an emotional hijacking of our thinking capacity, and people who would otherwise never be at risk for harming themselves or someone else may make irrational decisions because they are truly not in a rational place.

Bill's story is a prime example of an emotional hijacking. Bill and Angela were happily married with a cherished four-year-old daughter, Susan. They seemed to have a normal and happy life until they experienced a parent's worst nightmare when their little girl disappeared. Susan vanished while playing near their home, and it was a number of weeks before her body was discovered. Their worst fears were confirmed; she had been abducted, sexually assaulted, and brutally murdered. The situation was made worse in that the police never made an arrest in Susan's murder. While there was an outpouring of sympathy in the immediate days following the discovery of Susan's body, most people did not know what to say to the couple. As is commonly the case, this type of tragedy was painful for most people to think about, much less talk about, so Bill and Angela felt isolated and alone. Because it was so painful, they rarely even talked with each other about the tragedy. Unfortunately, their marriage could not withstand the impact of the trauma and ended in divorce.

Bill moved to another part of the state and started his life over. A few years later, he fell in love and married a wonderful woman named Kathy. While she knew about Bill's first marriage and the death of his little girl, she knew it was painful for him, so they didn't talk about it. Shortly after they married, they started a family of their own and had a son, Adam, and a daughter, Kelly. They seemed to have a good marriage and family. They were considered to be strong Christians and were active members of a local church. Bill was loved by his family, co-workers, neighbors, and members of his church and respected in the community. Years went by and Bill and Kathy's kids were now teenagers. Kathy noticed that Kelly began acting strangely the summer after her fourteenth birthday. Initially, she chalked it up to "normal teenage stuff." But Kelly became increasingly quiet. The normally outgoing and happy girl seemed withdrawn and depressed. She dressed differently and stopped spending time with her close friends. Concerned by what she was observing, Kathy confronted Kelly about the changes she was seeing and expressed her concern that something was wrong. Kelly disclosed to her mother that a close family friend and co-worker of Bill's had sexually molested her. This was very difficult for Kathy to hear, but she reassured Kelly that she had done the right thing in telling the truth and that her parents would protect her. Kathy sat down with Bill that evening when he got home from work to tell him the news and discuss how they should handle the situation. Bill was quiet when she told him that his friend had sexually molested their daughter. While she knew he was upset, he didn't show a strong emotional reaction. He was quiet and simply said, "OK, I understand." Kathy wanted to talk more about what they should do. Should they call the police? Should they talk to their pastor? Bill said they would talk about this later, but that he needed to go for a drive. Kathy did not see any reason to be concerned; she knew her husband. Anyone who knew Bill would tell you he was a rational and reasonable man. Kathy expected that he would take a drive to clear his head, then he would return home and they would discuss the best course of action to take to protect their daughter and to ensure that legal action was taken against the man who molested her. But neither Bill nor Kathy fully understood how trauma, past and present, was affecting Bill.

It is critical to understand what we discussed in the previous chapter regarding trauma and the brain to understand what occurred next. Instead of taking a drive to clear his head, Bill drove directly to the home of his "friend" who had molested his teenage daughter. When he arrived at the house, he found his friend working in the back yard. Bill shot and killed the man who had been accused of molesting his daughter, got back into his truck, and drove home. Later, Bill would admit that he had very little recollection of what had happened between the time he left his home and the time he arrived back home after shooting his friend. No one would have believed that Bill could have the capacity for murder. Even Bill would never have believed he could have committed this crime. But he wasn't thinking clearly or rationally. Blinded by the combined traumatic incidents of his dead and hurt daughters, he was functioning on a very basic drive to protect his daughter. The portion of his brain that could discern between right and wrong, the part of his brain that could understand the consequences of his actions and could determine the best course of action to protect his daughter, was impaired. Bill's amygdala was in control and that portion of the brain is driven by emotions, in this case, anger and fear.

Bill's response is an extreme case. Most trauma survivors do not behave in such an extreme manner. Most people who have experienced trauma or crisis situations do not commit murder, but a powerful rage and the desire to kill are commonly experienced and expressed by survivors. However, sometimes they do engage in behavior that can be very harmful to themselves or others. Like Bill, they may do or say things they would never do or say under ordinary circumstances. As crisis responders, we must be aware that one of the primary ways to provide safety for those in crisis is to keep them safe from themselves. We must be aware of the increased risks for homicidal or suicidal ideations in individuals who are in the midst of a psychological crisis. We must take any threats seriously and never assume that they "would never do something like that." We must also protect them from less immediate threats. Self-destructive behaviors such as substance abuse, high-risk sexual behaviors, or other high-risk behaviors such as driving too fast or putting themselves in dangerous situations can also be behavioral symptoms of posttraumatic stress. We need to be on the lookout for any way in which these individuals might harm themselves or others.

Sometimes crisis interveners focus too much on the emotional state of the survivor and fail even to assess if a survivor has sustained physical injuries. Ensuring physical safety involves encouraging individuals in crisis to seek medical assistance or to comply with the recommendations of medical professionals. In training crisis responders, we emphasize that when it comes to physical injuries or the potential need for medical assistance, it is always better to be safe than sorry. There have been incidents in which accident survivors leave the scene saying they feel fine and are not injured, only to collapse minutes or even hours later with serious internal injuries. In the acute aftermath of a critical incident, the body goes into a protective mode, and survivors may experience a rush of adrenaline and other chemicals that may mask injury and even pain.

When an officer and his partner stopped a car on the side of a rural Missouri highway, they had no idea that one of them would not leave the scene alive. Officer Jim watched as his partner walked to the driver's side of the stopped vehicle and fell when he was shot in the face. Officer Jim went into a self-protective state. He fired shots as the suspect fled the scene. He called for backup as he rushed to his comrade's side to try to save his life. It wasn't until later that he realized he had been shot in the shoulder. He stated that he didn't even feel pain for several days.

Because people in a state of crisis often experience diminished thinking capacity, they may make emotionally based decisions that can have a devastating long-term impact. One elderly woman, who witnessed a robbery, made a sudden decision to move to another location. Fortunately, someone intervened and had her stay with one of her children for a period of time while she processed what happened. As she talked about the incident, she changed her mind because she realized that it was an isolated incident that could have happened anywhere. She understood that her neighborhood crime statistics were far better than those almost anywhere else she could move. It would have been a huge loss for her to move and lose all the support, friends, and familiarity she had experienced for years, and to have to start all over somewhere else. Her family did the right thing by surrounding her with a loving presence and allowing her to talk about her fears, which helped her process the event and look at the situation objectively. Had they tried to change her mind just by reciting crime statistics without being present with her and listening to her fears, the outcome may have been different.

Feeling Safe

When I (Kevin) recovered from my accident and was in the emergency room, the medical staff had to first determine that I was stabilized and physically safe. They determined that I was not going to die, so they left me alone. However, the nurse saw in my eyes that I did not feel safe. The magnitude of the situation was just beginning to set in, and I was scared and feeling very alone. Well-meaning caregivers often fail to recognize how vulnerable survivors feel in the aftermath. Sometimes the reality of what has just occurred does not hit emotionally for several hours, days, or even weeks. Survivors may fall apart to the surprise of those around them who think they are "handling it well." It is important to help survivors understand that "falling apart" is really okay and that it doesn't mean that they aren't doing well. We must allow survivors to experience the full range of emotions without feeling that they need to act a certain way to appear to "be okay." Sometimes "not doing well" is what is needed; and if they are accepted by those around them, it can even help facilitate their healing journey. One of the most basic things you can do to help survivors is to ask, "Do you feel safe right now?" If they don't, ask them what could be done to help them feel safe.

Are You a Safe Person?

In John 8:1-11 there is a wonderful story in which Jesus provides safety for a woman brought before him who had been caught in the act of adultery. Trying to trap Jesus, they say she should be stoned for her sinful actions. Without answering them, Jesus calmly stoops to the ground and writes something in the dirt. They continue to argue with him, so again he stoops down and with his finger begins writing again while saying, "If any one of you is without sin, let him be the first to throw a stone at her" (NIV). Whatever he wrote must have been an incitement because each of them left, beginning with those who were oldest. Responding to an inquiry about where her accusers were, the woman said, "No one, sir." Jesus then says that neither does he condemn her and sends her on her way with the instructions to go and sin no more. In this story, Jesus takes command of the situation by acting in a calm way, perhaps saving both of their lives in the process. Even after her accusers leave, Jesus does not lecture or condemn her but rather gives her simple direction as he extends grace. People who hurt long for a church that seeks to create an environment of trust where they can find the protective arms of grace.

This leads us to an important element of consideration. As a crisis responder, are you a safe person? Being a safe person is absolutely critical when working with people in crisis. One of the most important things about helping people feel safe relates to confidentiality. After Jim and Dee began having marital problems and he got involved in an extramarital affair, two of Dee's friends independently approached her, saying that they were worried about her and felt that something was wrong. As she started crying, the story came out. One of them went to their small church and at the time of public prayer asked for prayer for some of her "best friends" who were having marital difficulties because the husband had been unfaithful. It wasn't difficult for anyone to figure out who it was. The other friend told her own husband even though Dee had asked her not to because neither Jim nor Dee trusted him. Both Jim and Dee felt violated and betrayed by the lack of confidentiality. The unintended consequence was that the couple then found it difficult to open up to others for help. Too often, the church becomes a rumor mill when members divulge confidential information under the guise of prayer requests. It is very important to talk about confidentiality right up front and get a person's permission before you share any information with another person.

The crisis responder must provide an environment of safety so that the individual in crisis feels able to experience pain, fear, anger, sadness, depression—whatever he or she is feeling. Individuals who experience crisis, trauma, and loss will frequently have a wide range of intense emotions and this can feel threatening and uncomfortable to some people. But they also need to be able to tell their story and experience these emotions with a person who will allow them to express them without judgment, fear, or denial. And most important, they need a person who will not try to fix them but rather will feel comfortable or at least at peace in the presence of their pain.

I (Jennifer) remember speaking with one man who had experienced a number of back-to-back traumatic events. As he was discussing all that had gone wrong and his resulting pain, he made the statement, "I just have to figure out how to hold it together." This is a strong message that most people who are experiencing pain and trauma get from the world and give to themselves. They feel they need to keep their emotions in check. They fear expressing their pain. They fear it will overwhelm them and that it will overwhelm others. My answer to this man was that perhaps instead of working so hard to "hold it together," he needed a safe place to fall apart. What would it mean to "fall apart," and why do people feel the need to "hold it together"? But a cautionary note: when you sense that a person is falling apart, please remember your own limitations. If you need additional help, seek a trained professional. If you are the trained professional, have the humility to seek out another professional colleague.

Quick Reference Tips for Meeting Safety Needs during the First 48 Hours

- Understand that survivors are particularly vulnerable in times of crisis.
- Remember that survivors are likely to have a reduced level of functioning and a diminished capacity to make good decisions to protect themselves and others.
- Assess whether they feel safe and take practical steps to help them feel safer.
- Make sure that they are surrounded by people who are safe people.

• Educate those who will be their primary support system on how to protect and keep them safe.

Think about This

1. If you have experienced a traumatic event, how did you feel in the aftermath?

2. Was there anything that happened after the event that made you feel even more unsafe?

3. What did others do that helped you feel safer?

4. How can the church help survivors feel safe within the scope of congregational care?

CHAPTER FOUR
Assessment and Triage

The question may often seem to be not *Who needs help?* but rather *Who doesn't need help?* The daily newscasts seem to depict unending stories of human suffering. Our mail boxes collect a continuous flow of appeal letters from organizations seeking funding to continue their work to help needy people. Most of these organizations are excellent, and we assist as much as we can and yet we can't support all of them and feel guilt that we cannot help more. Our homes and churches are filled with people struggling with difficulties that others may never know. Pastors too often feel overwhelmed by the constant needs of hurting people.

Pain and suffering are not new to society. We find them throughout the Bible. Cries of lament rise from the ground with the blood of Abel, and God takes notice and intervenes (Gen. 4:10). Yet Scripture also reveals that God cares for a suffering humanity as indicated in Psalm 103:6 (NIV), which states, "The LORD works righteousness / and justice for all the oppressed."

There is, then, a cosmic cycle of loss, pain, adversity, and death from which no one is spared. A multitude of other factors often exacerbates the impact of negative life events, adding to the complexity of integrating a traumatic situation or loss within a survivor's life. But negative life stressors must be addressed within one's perception of the world and one's existence within a hurting world. Sometimes the emotional and spiritual challenges are even more challenging than the negative life stressor. Powlison (2006) states, "Often the biggest problem for any sufferer is not 'the problem.' It is the spiritual challenge the problem presents" (p. 157). The church can play a critical role in helping people grow through these circumstances. However, there are just not enough helpers to come alongside everyone. Who do you help and where do you focus your efforts?

The Importance of Triage

It is common for paramedics and firefighters to arrive on the scene of an accident where there are multiple injured individuals; sometimes there are more victims than medical personnel. One of the first things emergency personnel must do is assess the situation and perform triage to ensure that they first provide medical care to the people who need it the most. A failure to recognize who needs care first can have a deadly outcome. Unless trained personnel understand what to assess, how to recognize important signs, and how to provide appropriate care, they may end up treating those who have only minor wounds while someone with severe internal damage goes unnoticed.

There is an old saying, "The squeaky wheel gets the grease." Medical personnel understand that the person screaming the loudest on scene may not be the one who is the most seriously injured. Those in charge of pastoral care in churches also know that sometimes the most demanding individuals can easily monopolize the caregivers' time. Experience has shown that sometimes the ones with the deepest wounds often go undetected because they suffer in silence.

There are those who want your time and those who truly need your help. Both Jennifer and I have coordinated the pastoral care and counseling ministries at several churches. There were always those people we referred to as "therapy campers." While there were issues in their lives that needed to be addressed, they often were not motivated to address these issues.

Critical Incidents and Development of a Crisis

A common mistake of crisis responders is to identify a particular, distressfully negative incident as a crisis. This can lead caregivers to falsely assume a state of crisis, which may not necessarily be true. A crisis occurs when a stressful incident overwhelms an individual's ability to cope effectively in the face of a perceived challenge or threat (Everly & Mitchell, 1999; Raphael, 1986). Thus, a survivor may experience a critical incident and yet never truly enter a state of crisis.

Caplan (1964) made a seminal contribution to the crisis intervention field with his emphasis on community mental health programs that focused on primary and secondary prevention. He was the first to describe the nature of a "psychological crisis" associated with a traumatic event. He clearly delineates a crisis as a response to an event rather than the distinguishing event itself.

Crisis responders should carefully assess a survivor's ability to cope in addition to other critical factors. A response to an event may be defined as a crisis when

1. psychological homeostasis (balance) has been disrupted;
2. one's usual coping mechanisms have failed to reestablish homeostasis; and
3. the distress engendered by the crisis has yielded some evidence of functional impairment (Caplan, 1961, 1964; Everly & Mitchell, 1999).

Traumatic events are extraordinary, not because of the rarity of occurrence, but rather because they overwhelm the ordinary human adaptations to life events. Traumatic events generally involve threats to one's own life or bodily integrity or a close personal encounter with violence and death. These encounters confront human beings with helplessness and terror and evoke a crisis response (Herman, 1997).

The *Comprehensive Textbook of Psychiatry* cites the common denominator of psychological trauma as a feeling of "intense fear, helplessness, loss of control, and threat of annihilation" (Andreasen, 1985).

Lawrenz and Green (1995) indicate that the following factors influence the stress impact of an event:

• The anticipation or experience of physical or psychological pain
• The experience of life changes (the more numerous the changes, the greater the stress)
• The cumulative amount of stressors in one's life
• Social support, such as friends and family (the less the support, the greater the perceived stress)

- Potential coping options or resources (the fewer the options or resources, the greater the perceived stress)
- Ambiguity or suddenness of the event
- The emotional and physical characteristics and present state of the individual

Common Reactions Experienced after a Traumatic Event

It is important to note that although individual reactions to stress, disasters, and traumatic events vary widely, clinical researchers identify a common pattern of behavioral, biological, psychological, spiritual, and social responses.

While the stress reactions that survivors may experience may seem "extreme" and may cause further distress, they generally do not become chronic problems. Research indicates that most people fully recover from moderate stress reactions within six to sixteen months.

Helping people understand that the following reactions are normal responses to an abnormal event can serve to greatly reduce their anxiety and worry when they experience these symptoms. When caregivers explain these normal reactions, it is common for people to quickly express relief that they are not "crazy after all." Mild to moderate stress reactions in the emergency and post-impact phases of disaster are highly prevalent because the affected individuals have accurately recognized the threat to their personal safety.

The following lists give common reactions of survivors. Please note that it is important that crisis responders understand these as normal reactions (Ellers, 2008).

Physical Effects

- Fatigue, exhaustion
- Increased physical pain
- Sleep disturbances
- Cardiovascular strain
- Reduced immune response
- Change in appetite
- Decreased libido
- Hyperarousal

- Nausea
- Dizziness
- Headaches
- Gastrointestinal problems
- Increased startle response
- Muscle tremors
- Profuse sweating
- Digestive problems
- Somatic complaints
- Ritualistic behavior
- More accident prone

Emotional Effects

- Shock
- Fear/terror
- Irritability
- Anger
- Grief or sadness
- Depression
- Despair
- Loss of pleasure from familiar activities
- Nervousness
- Blame
- Guilt
- Emotional numbing
- Helplessness
- Identification with the victim
- Difficulty feeling happy

Interpersonal Effects

- Increased relational conflict
- Reduced relational intimacy
- Impaired work performance
- Impaired school performance
- Feeling abandoned/rejected
- Social withdrawal
- Alienation
- Decreased satisfaction

- Distrust
- Externalization of blame
- Externalization of vulnerability
- Overprotectiveness

Cognitive Effects

- Impaired concentration
- Impaired decision-making ability
- Memory impairment
- Disbelief
- Confusion
- Distortion
- Self-blame
- Decreased self-esteem
- Decreased self-efficacy
- Worry
- Dissociation (e.g., tunnel vision, or a dreamlike or "spacey" feeling)

Spiritual Effects

- Spiritual disconnection from God
- Questioning God and theological beliefs
- Anger at God
- Spiritual emptiness
- Withdrawal from the faith community
- Increased awareness of mortality
- Guilt for feelings, e.g., anger, desire for vengeance

Problematic Stress Responses

It is vital for you to watch for signs that survivors may need to be referred to mental health services. The following responses indicate the likelihood of an individual's need for mental health assessment and care (adapted from: *Effects of Traumatic Stress in a Disaster Situation: A National Center for PTSD Fact Sheet*):

- *Severe dissociation* (feeling as though you or the world is "unreal," not feeling connected to one's own body, losing one's sense of identity or taking on a new identity, amnesia)

- *Severe intrusive reexperiencing* (flashbacks, terrifying screen memories or nightmares, repetitive automatic reenactment)
- *Extreme avoidance* (agoraphobic-like social or vocational withdrawal, compulsive avoidance)
- *Severe hyperarousal* (panic episodes, terrifying nightmares, difficulty controlling violent impulses, inability to concentrate)
- *Debilitating anxiety* (ruminative worry, severe phobias, unshakeable obsessions, paralyzing nervousness, fear of losing control / "going crazy")
- *Severe depression* (lack of pleasure in life, feelings of worthlessness, self-blame, dependency, early awakenings, persistent fatigue, lack of motivation)
- *Problematic substance use* (abuse or dependency, self-medication)
- *Psychotic symptoms* (delusions, hallucinations, bizarre thoughts or images)

Bolin (1989) summarizes with five key points. First, critical incidents that expose victims to life-threatening situations or to the death or injury of a friend or family member are more likely to produce psychological distress. Second, disaster agents that are accompanied by long periods of danger or the threat of recurrence after an initial intense impact may be particularly stressful. In general, post-impact threat of recurrence will be more stressful than pre-impact stress. As noted earlier, earthquakes, volcanic eruptions, and tornadoes are frequently accompanied by threats of recurrence (Bolin & Bolton, 1986; Leik et al., 1982). This is one reason that critical incidents that involve human intent or negligence exacerbate the impact, because there is higher recognition of vulnerability. Third, when combined with an intense impact, disasters with a high ratio of damaged to undamaged community are associated with adverse mental health outcomes. This includes earthquakes, some flood events, and major tornadoes. Fourth, critical incidents with a sudden and unanticipated onset will be more stressful than anticipated events (Quarantelli, 1985). Fifth, critical incidents with which victims are unfamiliar are more likely to be psychologically disturbing. Previous experience with similar threats, individually or collectively, may help mitigate the stress effects of the threatening agent associated with the critical incident (Mileti et al., 1975).

Acute Stress Disorder (ASD) and Posttraumatic Stress Disorder (PTSD)

A number of symptoms are normal in the wake of crisis and trauma. Any person who experiences an event that threatens his or her life, safety, or well-being or who witnesses an event in which someone is injured or killed will likely experience a set of physical, cognitive, behavioral, or spiritual symptoms. These symptoms, when experienced in the immediate aftermath of a crisis event, are not pathological and should be normalized. Explanation and normalization of these symptoms is a significant aspect of crisis intervention. However, it is the severity and duration of these symptoms that can indicate the presence of an anxiety disorder such as ASD or PTSD.

Acute Stress Disorder

ASD is a psychiatric diagnosis that can be given to individuals in the first month following a traumatic event. The symptoms that define ASD overlap with those for PTSD, although there are a greater number of dissociative symptoms for ASD, such as not knowing where you are or feeling as if you are outside of your body. Because ASD is a relatively new diagnosis, research on the disorder is in the early stages. To be diagnosed with ASD individuals must have three or more of the following dissociative symptoms:

1. Subjective sense of numbing, detachment, or absence of emotional responsiveness
2. A reduction in awareness of his or her surroundings
3. Derealization
4. Depersonalization
5. Dissociative amnesia

ASD is also characterized by persistent reexperiencing of the event, avoidance of stimuli that bring back memories of the trauma, and marked symptoms of anxiety such as sleeplessness, irritability, and hypervigilance. ASD can be diagnosed only within the first thirty days following the event. A diagnosis of ASD appears to be a strong predictor of subsequent PTSD. In one study, more than three-quarters of individuals who were in motor vehicle accidents and met criteria for ASD went on to develop PTSD (Bryant & Harvey, 2000). This finding is consistent with other studies that found that over 80 percent of people with ASD had developed PTSD by the time they were assessed six months later (Creamer and Manning, 1998; Bryant, Guthrie & Moulds, 2001).

Posttraumatic Stress Disorder

If Posttraumatic Stress symptoms persist for longer than thirty days, the diagnosis of PTSD can be given. Although there is considerable variation among factors, it has been estimated that 5-11 percent of trauma victims will develop PTSD (Breslau, 2001). Symptoms include:

1. Reexperiencing the event through intrusive thoughts or dreams and intense distress upon exposure to any stimulus or cue that causes the individual to recall the event.
2. Avoidance of stimuli associated with the trauma and numbing of general responsiveness through efforts to avoid thoughts, feelings, or conversations associated with the trauma, as well as avoidance of anything that triggers recollection of the trauma. Individuals may also experience an inability to recall certain aspects of the event, diminished interest in significant activities, feelings of detachment from other people, a restricted range of affect, and a sense of a foreshortened future.
3. Individuals may also experience symptoms such as sleep disturbances, irritability or anger, difficulty concentrating, hypervigilance, and exaggerated startle response.
4. If the symptoms persist between thirty days and three months, the PTSD is acute. If duration of the symptoms is three months or more, the PTSD is considered chronic.

While the impact of a critical incident is always personal, one must also understand that the trauma will likely manifest itself in the stress and grief reactions of survivors and may significantly affect relationships.

Stages of Posttrauma and Family Systems

Not only must caregivers assess an individual's response to trauma, one must consider that individuals live within systems, which can have a significant impact on how survivors cope with adversity. As we all know, advances in technology contribute to a mobile, isolated, and disconnected society. When survivors are asked who the people closest to them are, they may point to family, friends, and coworkers. It is not uncommon for people to spend far more time with coworkers than with family members and thus to feel far more emotionally connected to them.

Families are also systems of relationships. These must be considered as well. Johnson (1989) discusses posttrauma responses of survivors in three stages as they relate to the family system: recoil, reorganization, and restabilization.

Recoil

Following a critical incident, the family may initially respond by aligning themselves to meet the threat. There may be a feeling of closeness during this time. This may be referred to as the second honeymoon. One may find that there is an increased sense of intimacy, trust, and communication. Even long-standing conflicts and resentments are typically suspended temporarily as the system is affected.

Reorganization

In this stage, as the situation stabilizes, one may find that old patterns of communication, conflicts, and role relationships reassert themselves with the increased stress of the crisis. As discussed earlier, a family may become stronger or may drift toward increased polarization, differentiation, and fragmentation. Family members who have already been adversely affected by the trauma may feel increased isolation accentuated by the recent increase in family solidarity.

Restabilization

If family members are unable to rebuild the relationships exactly as before, the system may settle into a new period of stability characterized by deteriorated or increased levels of intimacy, affection, communication, and trust. It is in this period that family members are challenged to gain new strength or risk family deterioration.

It is important to help survivors identify key support systems in their lives. Take a few minutes to list some of the support systems you have found to be helpful to people in crisis and trauma.

Stress and Resiliency

All individuals and families experience stress. However, when looking at families who experience similar events, one readily observes that families face these situations in very different ways and demonstrate a wide range of reactions. While some families are able to bear great adversity and appear to adapt well to a critical incident, no two families have the same stressors associated with any event regardless of how it may appear to an external observer. In reviewing the research, we find that there are multifaceted determinants of each family's coping ability. However, one's response largely depends upon a person's subjective interpretation of the critical incident or stressor.

Some of the most helpful material on families in crisis comes from family stress theory (Patterson & Garwick, 1994). The earliest work in this area was Reuben Hill's ABCX family crisis model (Hill, 1958). This model was later adapted into the Double ABCX Model of Adjustment and Adaptation (McCubbin & Patterson, 1983). This expanded model not only looks at the precrisis variables but also adds postcrisis variables and the accumulation of additional stressors that families may experience. The three facets in this expanded model are the family member, the family, and the family's community (McCubbin & Patterson, 1983).

Too often we forget to assess the extended support system that a person has and may therefore try to link the person with a non-supportive system. A crisis response chaplain was working with a man who was feeling suicidal. The chaplain kept trying to get the man to consider the impact that his death would have on his wife and was trying to get him to allow his wife to support him. However, the chaplain had not taken the time to assess what was so bad about his life that he would want to end it, nor had the chaplain assessed who in the man's life would be most supportive. The chaplain felt unsuccessful in providing help to the suicidal man. A little later, as the man's father was talking with the chaplain, the picture became clear. The father painted a picture of a difficult marriage in which the man's wife had been very emotionally unstable and abusive. The husband felt trapped and isolated from the rest of the family, who felt that he allowed her to control his life in a very unhealthy way. After hearing this information, the chaplain changed his approach because directing this man to look to his wife for support was absolutely unhelpful. One of the greatest mistakes that we tend to make as caregivers is to jump to conclusions without carefully assessing the reality of a situation. Life is far more complex than it often appears, and caregivers' attempts to provide easy answers can fail to help people find ways to make it through the difficult times.

Navigating the Post-incident Aftermath

It is important to note that in addition to the stress of the incident, there are secondary stresses that are response-generated demands (Quarantelli, 1985). For example, in disasters a caregiver may hear survivors indicate that even though they were afraid at the time of the tornado and suffered a loss, they are currently not suffering any psychological disturbances. However, they may indicate a huge amount of stress surrounding the aftermath of the disaster in trying to navigate the complex system of obtaining help through governmental and nongovernmental agencies. It is important that the caregiver be aware of this, because apparent psychological stress may be mitigated by information. A failure to identify the source of the individual's stress may produce an ineffective ministry response.

A common theme in the way people respond to stressors is their perception of what is outside the bounds of their control. This is particularly relevant to the disaster worker and the specific stressors that he or she will encounter on the disaster scene. What is most critical is how survivors *perceive* the impact of the event and whether resources to meet the added demand. Caregivers can play a critical role in building resiliency and enhancing existing social support systems.

The Stress Cycle

Critical incidents often place increased levels of stress on existing systems. However, "Stress is the result of personal investment in difficult situations. If no investment exists, there is no basis for stress" (Johnson, 1989). As beauty is in the eye of the beholder, so is one's view of critical incidents.

It is normal to assume that stressful situations directly cause our stress reactions. Yet investigations of the dynamics of stress-related problems show that these problems are best understood in terms of unsuccessful coping cycles. Each stage is a reaction to the overall situation, but it also serves to set up the next stage. Because each stage represents an escalation of stress, adversely affecting the total situation, this process is cyclical in nature. Johnson identified three stages of stress, which follow.

Stage One: Expectations

This stage consists of a situation and the individual's expectations. If the expectations are reasonable and realistic, there is a better chance of successful coping than if expectations are unrealistic and unreasonable.

Stage Two: Appraisal

In stage two, the situation is evaluated for type and projected outcome. Three styles of appraisal can destine the situation to failure. First, certain types of judgments are self-defeating. Black-and-white thinking, preoccupations, categorical and absolutist judgments, overgeneralizations, and "looking for the negative" can place the entire situation in an unworkable, pessimistic light. Second, a self-fulfilling bias may cause a person to concentrate on information that confirms preexisting beliefs and to ignore information that contradicts those beliefs. The result is obvious—the person's subsequent experiences confirm the preexisting beliefs. Third, the appraisal stage may create stress due to a person's negative set of beliefs. Habitual beliefs, assumptions, and commitments influence the way one interprets situations. Past experiences and emotional vulnerabilities can lock people into negative ways of viewing and responding to the world. Everly (1989) states, "Practically speaking, there is simply no such thing as 'reality' without considering the human perspective that might be brought to bear upon it" (p. 25).

Stage Three: Internal Dialogue

An internal dialogue can serve to reinforce the negative appraisal and expectation set, compounding a person's reaction to perceived stressors. This is the third stage of the stress cycle. Not only can the person experience the world in a needlessly negative way, but he or she may repeat such self-messages as "Nothing ever goes right," "God is out to get me again," "I should know better than to try; something bad always will happen when I do," or "You blew it again, you stupid fool." Such thoughts arise almost spontaneously and influence the way a person interprets and predicts events. Negative thoughts automatically affect how individuals feel about situations and may create further negative situations. Clinicians frequently refer to this negative thought pattern as "stinking thinking." These negative thought patterns can serve to increase the stress response levels in addition to impairing positive coping mechanisms.

Stage Four: Emotional Response

In this stage emotional response occurs in reaction to not only external events but also the expectations, appraisals, and automatic thoughts accompanying the events. When a person has perceived and appraised a situation as threatening and has listened to automatic thoughts giving negative messages, he or she tends to react emotionally and to get upset. The nervous system goes into the "fight or flight" response. This starts the complex physiological arousal process that leads to emergency behavior and further emotional upset.

The key to dealing with the emotional response to a stressful situation is to become aware of it and manage it before it becomes unmanageable. Early awareness buys time to change thought patterns, to leave the situation, to take action to change the situation, or to work at modifying the physiological response itself.

Physiologically, the relaxation response is incompatible with the arousal response; hence, techniques that increase relaxation tend to decrease emotionality. Getting away, controlling breathing, exercising, and counting to ten are active ways to break the stress response cycle.

Stage Five: Response

The fifth stage is the actual response to the situation. How a person responds affects the situation positively or negatively. Responses are shaped by the appraisal, expectations, and cognitive and emotional processes in the overall interpretation of the event. To the extent those processes have been negative, a person is set up for a negative response. The resulting behaviors then contribute to a disintegrating situation. A thorough assessment of stress reactions would need to include an assessment of each of the stress cycle stages discussed above (Johnson, 1989).

In the stress cycle we can readily recognize the impact of negative thinking and appraisal patterns. However, it is important to note that positive patterns of appraisal and cognitive dialogue can have a powerful impact upon how we react to stressors. Hans Selye, who is known as the father of modern endocrinology, has summarized over fifty years of research related to stress with the conclusion, "It is not what happens to you that matters, but how you take it" (Everly 1989).

Stress versus Crisis

We commonly find people equating the terms "stress" and "crisis" and using them interchangeably. While both stress and crisis involve discomfort, these two concepts are often confused. Here is a set of guidelines to help you tell the difference (Slaikeu, 1990):

1. The coping patterns arising during crisis are different from those associated with stress. Coping during crisis seems to be more "personal," involving fewer nuclear family and informal supports.
2. During the crisis state, the individual tends to be less defensive and more open to suggestions, influence, and

support (Halpern, 1973), though this is not characteristically true of stress.

3. The outcome of crisis can be either debilitation or growth. Stress, on the other hand, is usually associated with pathology and has as its most optimistic outcome adaptation to the wear and tear caused by life's circumstances or return to the status quo (Selye, 1976).

Crisis occurs over a relatively short period of time (about six weeks), whereas stress does not have this self-limiting quality. Stress is more often viewed as a chronic condition building over time, whereas a crisis is associated with a sudden onset.

Survivor Resiliency Factors

In the impact stage following a disaster or traumatic event, disaster workers and caregivers can serve to provide a buffer for individuals by providing comfort, safety, and clear thinking. This is an instance where the well-worn phrase that "two heads are better than one" applies.

Richard Davidson, the director of the Laboratory for Affective Neuroscience at the University of Wisconsin, conducted a landmark study of brain imaging that tested two groups of people. One group was identified as highly resistant to life's ups and downs and the other as easily upset by them. Davidson tracked participants' brain function as they performed stressful tasks. The research revealed that resilient people had a remarkably fast recovery from stress, with their prefrontal areas starting to calm the amygdala and themselves within seconds. By contrast, the more vulnerable people showed a continued escalation of their amygdala's activity and their perceived distress for several minutes after the activity ended (Sherman, 1994; Goleman, 1998).

Davidson found that the resilient people had already started to inhibit the distress during the stressful encounter. He identified these people as optimistic, action-oriented people. These individuals faced life's stressors by immediately trying to make things better. A study of store managers at a large American retail chain found that the managers who were most tense, beleaguered, or overwhelmed by job pressures ran stores with the worst performance, as measured by net profits, sales per square foot, sales per employee, and sales per dollar of inventory investment. Interestingly, those who stayed the most composed under the same pressures had the best per-store sales records (Sherman, 1994).

Assessing the Perception of Control

A survivor's perception of control not only plays a powerful role in how he or she copes in the aftermath of a critical incident, it also plays a significant role in the stress cycle. This is discussed further in other sections of the book.

Positive Outcome of Negative Life Events

There seems to be a tendency to focus on the negative impacts of traumatic events and loss. As practitioners, we have observed that traumatic events and negative life stressors, while oftentimes stressful and having short-term negative impact, can also present long-term positive growth and development. Growing evidence supports the concept that the long-term outcome of negative life events can lead to posttraumatic growth. Therefore, as crisis responders, we must make a conscious effort to assess and highlight survivor resiliency factors (Ellers, 2008).

A national survey of 1,481 participants asked how often a death in the family strengthened the religious faith of the respondent. The study found that 66 percent of the respondents answered "often" or "sometimes" (Davis & Smith, 1995). Several different studies indicate an increased religious faith in cancer patients, varying from 15-39 percent (Reed, 1987; O'Connor, Wicker, & Germino, 1990; Curbow, et al., 1993).

Some studies indicate an increased religious faith in people who had experienced the death of a loved one: a spouse or child 15 percent (Lehman, et al., 1993); college students with the death of a parent or close relative, 30 percent (Schwartzberg & Janoff-Bulman, 1991) and 25 percent (Edmonds & Hooker, 1992). In a study of severely ill adolescents, age 11-19, almost 50 percent had increased spiritual concerns (Silber & Reilly, 1985). These studies revealed that the highest rates, from 25-50 percent, were found in studies that asked questions specifically about religion, while the lower rates came from studies that asked general open-ended questions about the effects of traumatic experience. This research clearly indicates the critical role that the church can fill in providing for the emotional and spiritual needs of survivors and encouraging growth and development following traumatic events.

Assessing a Survivor's Perception of Impact and Resources

The purpose of this book is to help prepare caregivers to come alongside people in the immediate aftermath of a critical incident and provide essential care. Providing care in the immediately following critical incidents can have a beneficial long-term impact that is often not recognized. It is critical that caregivers be able to come alongside survivors in this immediate aftermath as survivors often have diminished capacity to make sound decisions and frequently do not consider important factors that may have numerous adverse long-term effects.

In the early aftermath of a critical incident there are several important elements for crisis responders to assess. Again, the most important component of this is the perception that the survivor has about his or her situation. Too often, we enter the world of the survivor with our own preconceived ideas of how the critical incident has impacted their lives, which may be totally wrong.

A few years ago, I (Kevin) was working with a disaster response team outside the Kansas City area. A tornado had ripped through a suburban community leaving a broad path of destruction. A church had miraculously been spared in the middle of the impact zone, and people congregated there for disaster relief services. Serving as a chaplain on the disaster relief team, I spent time going from table to table talking with people as they ate their meals. As I sat with one family, they talked with great animation about the impact that the tornado had on made them. They had sustained minor damage to their home, but the tornado had disrupted their lives by forcing them to take time from work. It was clear that they were worried about their finances. After a while, they thanked me for listening and said that they thought they were going to be okay. However, before I left, they pointed to an elderly man sitting at another table and said I should talk with him because he had lost everything, and they were worried about him. His wife had died a few years before, and none of his children lived in the area. I left them and immediately went to talk with him. After introducing myself, I told him how sorry I was that he had lost everything. I went on to say that I couldn't imagine how hard it was to sustain such a loss so soon after his wife had died. As I talked, he sat quietly eating his food and not saying much. After a while, I said to him. "You know I am making a lot of assumptions about how this has impacted your life. How has it impacted you?" After looking down at his food for a little while, he looked up at me with a twinkle in his eye and said, "I didn't like that old house anyway." Once I finally shut up and actually listened to him, he told me that his children lived in different parts of the country. After his wife had died, he had thought many times about moving, but he just didn't know what to do with all the stuff they had accumulated, and he didn't have the energy to move everything and wasn't really sure what to do with it all anyway. He was well insured and had a substantial amount of savings. For him, his problems were now solved. He said that he would miss a few things, but overall he felt free to travel and be with his children more.

I learned a valuable lesson from this situation. Too often we caregivers go from person to person without ever wiping our perception slate clean. While the man had sustained significant physical loss in the eyes of the outside world, the impact on his life was far less than that of his neighbors, who had sustained much less actual physical damage. Too often we assess a higher level of emotional and spiritual impact than may actually be present. When caregivers make this mistake, they can interfere with the survivor's God-given, natural coping mechanisms and cause harm. We need to help people make a realistic assessment of their situation, while at the same time evaluating the resources they bring to help them cope with the critical incident. As one survivor of Hurricane Katrina stated, "When you train your emotional and spiritual care teams, tell them not to bring their 'poor you' mentality down here with them. We have enough sadness and despair here as it is. Deal with your own issues; bring us happiness and hope. Laugh with us and inspire us."

Three Dimensions for Assessment of a Survivor's Perception

It is critical that emotional and spiritual caregivers assess three critical dimensions of a survivor's perception in the immediate aftermath of a critical incident. When caregivers carefully complete this assessment, they are more likely to meet survivors where they are, survivors will feel heard and validated, and caregivers can ensure that survivors receive the care that they need.

There are three important issues that emotional and spiritual caregivers need to assess: (1) How the survivor perceives the critical incident; (2) How the survivor perceives his or her available resources; and (3) How the survivor perceives the personal impact. This can be done very simply and quickly with people in times of crisis and can provide an environment of empathic listening, exploration, and assessment of the impact; can help survivors identify coping resources; and can help survivors determine how they can help themselves as well as invite the help of caring communities to sustain them through the aftermath. The three things to assess are the perception the survivor has of the critical incident, available resources, and the impact on the survivor.

How Does the Survivor Perceive the Critical Incident?

One of the first things I have learned to do is to explore how survivors view the critical incident. This is very important for several reasons. The survivors may not see the critical incident as having made a significant impact on their lives. A rookie fire chaplain was sent in by the fire administration and local political authorities to provide care after a response in which a woman had been badly mangled and killed in a car accident. This event had had a very powerful impact on sections of the community, as the woman had been known and loved by many. The firefighters who had responded finally asked the chaplain why he was hanging around so much. One of the responders said, "Chaplain, are you hanging around here because of that woman that died?" He noted that this was the case and said that he wanted to make sure they were okay. They said "We are all fine!" Fortunately, they were. There are some events that would always trigger these seasoned firefighters, and there were some that would not significantly affect them. What may seem like a significant critical incident to one person may not to another. People are often surprised by who is affected by what.

How Does the Survivor Perceive the Available Resources?

It is very important to explore a survivor's perception of the resources they have that will help them meet the stressors of the critical incident. Often in the middle of a potential crisis state, survivors underestimate the resources upon which they can draw. Regardless of how many resources a survivor actually has, in the shock of overwhelming life events, he or she may not perceive there to be adequate internal and external resources. If this is the case, it can significantly increase the potential for a survivor to enter into a crisis state. The perception of adequate resources to meet the added demands of the critical incident can play an important role in mitigating a crisis state. There are a number of things that caregivers can do to help the survivor assess existing resources and cope with the critical incident.

Sometimes you may perceive that survivors have few resources available to them, but survivors may actually think that their resources are plentiful. We found this to be the case after Hurricane Katrina. We were coordinating a number of crisis response teams at different sites along the Gulf Coast that were ministering to volunteers and survivors. We had been working with survivors in Perlington, Mississippi, a very small town that had been at the point of the storm's entry, and the entire town had been destroyed. There was an amazing level of resiliency in the town's residents, who had created a tent village on a piece of property that had almost dried out, and volunteer teams were giving support to the residents. Eventually, the residents began receiving small, used travel trailers, which seemed like mansions compared to the tents. A new group of volunteers came down to help from a very influential area and were shocked and appalled by the cramped living quarters and the neighborhood. As well-intentioned as they were, they ended up causing more psychological harm than good as they subconsciously conveyed their perceptions to the survivors, who prior to their coming had felt they were doing pretty well. I talked with one of the residents later about the training program we had employed for our emotional and spiritual care teams. I asked her what she would like us to teach to these teams in preparing them to assist survivors. She said, "Please tell them not to come down here with their 'poor you' mentality. Bring happiness, bring joy, bring a positive outlook. We have enough difficulty and sadness without having to deal with their own sadness from not being able to deal with our pain." Sometimes, we can subconsciously have an adverse impact on people through our actions and behaviors, and we need to be very careful with how we approach people. Even the questions we ask can powerfully influence a person's perception.

Caregivers should explore the following:

Internal resources. Internal coping resources are those that reside within the survivor and can include a number of things. Some things to explore are physical, psychological, emotional, and spiritual health. These internal coping resources are critical. Looking for signs of resiliency is an important part of this process. Some questions to explore are:

- What are some of the things that have gotten you through tough situations in the past?
- Where do you get your strength to make it through tough times?
- How were you doing before this event happened?

External resources. External support resources come from outside the survivor and can include many things that might not be considered without exploration. I often start with a circle in the middle of a piece of paper and write "you" in the center of it. I draw spokes out from the circle with small circles on the ends. Using this diagram, I brainstorm with the survivor different external resources he or she may have. I look for people, places, and things. After Sally's rape, she felt that God gave her a special cat to help facilitate healing in her life. This cat was her constant companion and seemed to be able to sense the innermost sorrow of her soul. This cat came alongside her in a safe way that was very comforting. This safe, loving, accepting, and nonjudging relationship got her through that excruciating experience, along with many other things she would experience through the years. Many people would not have recognized or acknowledged how much of a physical and emotional support this cat was to her.

We let survivors start listing what they can think of. This tells me what things come to mind first and can be very revealing about how connected they are with others. We often find that initially they may not be able to identify many things. The important thing for caregivers to do is to ask questions to help survivors discover and name those resources that are helpful to them. Again, we need to make sure that we don't fall into the trap of doing all of the thinking for them and presuming to lecture them about resources that could be helpful to them.

How Does the Survivor Perceive the Personal Impact?

The third thing that crisis responders need to look at is how the survivor perceives the personal impact of the critical incident. I (Kevin) never cease to be amazed at how two people who experience a similar situation can have totally different perspectives. This was highlighted by a situation that happened early this morning as I was writing this chapter. This has been a brutally cold winter in Chicago, and the subzero temperatures and snow have seemed to be relentless. One of the things that I love to do is walk, and I typically walk most weekday evenings before going to bed, and on the weekend I rise early and walk. Yesterday was the first day in months that actually seemed warm, as it got up to 50 degrees, which is great for February. This morning, excited by the melting snow from yesterday, I was outside by 7:00 a.m. I got my motorcycle out for a ride later in the morning. As I made my way through the neighborhood, I was deep in thought and prayer, having a wonderful time walking with God. I saw a woman coming toward me and joyfully said, "Good morning, another beautiful day!" She started laughing and said, "Yeah!" and went on her way. As I walked another few blocks, it hit me that she wasn't agreeing with me; she was saying, "Yeah, right!" I looked around and realized that the sun was not shining, and it was actually quite dreary and cloudy. When I got home, I checked the temperature and it was only 33 degrees. After the weeks of subzero temperatures and piles of snow, it seemed warm. Because of my wonderful time with God, my soul had been enlightened from within, and I hadn't really paid much attention to the external conditions. For a brief period after my encounter with the woman, I started to gripe about the cloudy day. Then I realized what was going on. Later that morning, no longer affected by the woman's perception, I laughed as I rode my motorcycle by the lake on the way to church and observed several guys, all bundled in their clothes, ice fishing. Sometimes in the winter of our lives we have faced so much adversity that it almost becomes normal. We develop a certain level of psychological resistance to things and this can serve us positively. Make sure that as a crisis responder you do not do anything to negatively impact a survivor's perception or natural coping mechanisms.

How a survivor perceives the first two factors will influence how he or she perceives the level of personal impact. If survivors perceive that they have a sufficient level of internal and external resources to meet the stressors created by the critical incident, then it is less likely that they will perceive the impact to be high. However, if they perceive that they have few resources with which to meet what they perceive to be a critical incident that is a high stressor, then they will likely perceive that the personal impact on them is greater. The presence of all three—high stress, a low level of coping resources, and high personal impact—is the situation most likely to produce a state of crisis for the survivor.

Getting through Today and Preparing for Tomorrow

In the early aftermath of a traumatic event, a common mistake is to try to get survivors to look to the past or project too far into the future. Remember that one of the basics in the early aftermath of a critical incident is to stabilize the situation and deal only with the crisis at hand. You have to keep things simple and understand that in times of crisis, survivors often have a diminished capacity to think clearly and objectively. The event may bring up traumas from the past that may need to be dealt with at some time in the future, but the early aftermath is not the time to focus on the past. At this time it is critical to carefully assess what will bring stability to the survivor and his or her family and help get them through the day. However, it doesn't mean that one doesn't think about the future. There is a tendency for survivors to make rash decisions in the immediate aftermath of a critical incident that can have significant long-term negative consequences.

I (Kevin) have worked extensively with disaster survivors through the years. I never cease to be amazed at the broad variance in perception that I find within different geographic, cultural, and socioeconomic areas. I have learned to approach each individual within a disaster area as if I have had no prior disaster experience with other survivors. Otherwise, I tend to jump to conclusions. The levels of coping and resilience and victimization cannot be defined by culture or race or socioeconomic status. While I sometimes do find some patterns in how people cope within cultures, this is not always true. For example, I have often found that disaster survivors from rural farm communities tend to be more self-sufficient and are often more reluctant to seek the help of outsiders. They do not typically feel a sense of entitlement that someone will take care of them. In fact, there have been some disasters where funds have been donated to assist in rural areas, but the survivors have been very reluctant to accept any outside funds. Through the years, however, I have found many people from rural areas to have been open and willing to accept outside assistance, and I have seen people from urban areas who have been just as independent and closed to outside assistance. Again, the importance is to wipe your slate clean and start with a new slate every time you work with another survivor. God has designed each individual as a unique person, and each of us has many experiences through the years that have significantly shaped who we are and how we view the world. Our task as crisis responders is to meet survivors where they are and walk with them as they explore new ways of rebuilding their lives. In summary, always assess; never assume. Remember that you often find what you are looking for and what you expect to find. If you only look for the negative signs, you will likely find them. However, if you look for signs of resiliency and hope, you will also likely find them. The challenge is to realistically and objectively assess the individual and his or her situation, and to explore what would be of greatest assistance in helping survivors make it through that early period. What happens in the first few days can have a long-term impact on the survivor and can greatly shape his or her recovery process.

Assessing Loss Issues

In this chapter we have talked a lot about assessing the psychological and physical impacts of critical incidents. However, sometimes a person is affected most at the emotional level, but the individual may not experience any debilitating psychological symptoms. It can be confusing as what may seem to be a major critical incident or loss can be weathered with minimal visible impact while another incident that may seem less problematic can trigger significant levels of distress. One of the things that research and past experience have taught us is that it is important to assess the level of perceived loss that survivors experience. One day as I (Kevin) was talking with one of my best volunteers, I asked him how he was doing. He had been talking about how his mother-in-law who had lived with them for many years and with whom he had a very close relationship had recently died. I commented that this must have been a difficult loss for him and his wife. He said it was an adjustment, but in his words she was "pretty old and in bad health and her death was, I hate to say, a blessing for her." As we talked for a while, I asked how other things in his life were going. He mentioned that his mother-in-law's death had left a huge hole in their family unit. He had recently retired and, because of poor health, had not been able to volunteer as much as he had before, and he missed it. As we talked, I pointed out that he had had a lot of losses, and he opened up and began speaking about how this had affected him. I asked him what else was going on in his life. He got tears in his eyes and said that the hardest thing he was struggling with was that Dixie had died; my mind raced to remember who Dixie was. But as he went on talking, I realized that he was talking about his dog. Some people would not have recognized the importance that his four-legged companion had in his life and consequently may have missed the significance of this loss. Likely this loss was even more compounded by the loss of his mother-in-law. It is critical to understand the nature of a crisis and to recognize a person's perception of a critical incident. In the immediate aftermath, survivors are often unaware of the levels of loss that they have experienced, but this will become increasingly clear to them as time goes on. If the crisis responder will be working with a survivor long-term, he or she will likely have many opportunities to address the grief and loss issues with people. Addressing the losses that people experience in critical incidents is important. These losses can have profound long-term effects on survivors if the losses are not acknowledged and the survivors do not understand the impact of these losses and do not learn how to grieve them in a way that is helpful for the recovery process.

Quick Reference Tips for Assessment during the First 48 Hours

- Assess the basic needs of the survivors and take practical steps to help meet those needs.
- Remember to assess any physical damage.
- Assess traumatic elements to which the survivor may have been exposed.
- Assess the survivors' perception about the critical incident. Do they see it as traumatic event or as just a stressor?
- Assess how the survivors perceive their available resources.
- Assess how the survivors perceive the personal impact.
- Don't assume that survivors will have adverse long-term impacts.
- Look for ways to foster resiliency in the survivors and to help them sustain emotional and spiritual growth through the adversity.
- Assess the survivors' social support system and take steps to connect them with a good ongoing support system.
- Assess how you can help educate people within the survivor's social support system as to what signs and symptoms to watch for and how to help survivors cope.

Think about This

1. Can you think of a time when someone you knew experienced something you thought would have a very negative impact but appeared to have a minimal impact, and the person never seemed to experience a state of crisis?

2. What can the church do to build resiliency in the body of believers?

3. As you reviewed the commonly experienced signs and symptoms of posttrauma stress, did you see any that you have experienced yourself?

4. If you experienced these things, how did this impact you?

5. What did people do to help assess your situation and provide care?

How We Help: Practical Assistance in Crisis Response

What Is Crisis Intervention?

People are often apprehensive about going to the aid of someone in crisis because they do not know what to say or do. However, in the early aftermath of a critical incident, it is often the simple things that are most helpful and effective in getting survivors through the impact stage. Here is a brief overview of the basics.

Crisis Intervention and Disaster Mental Health Care

Disaster mental health care was birthed from the field of crisis intervention. For frontline crisis response organizations, crisis response concepts have served as the basis for valuable training for staff and volunteers. The primary goal of crisis intervention is to assist individuals in returning to an adaptive level of functioning and to mitigate the adverse impact and in particular, the psychological trauma of a critical incident (Everly & Mitchell, 1999).

The modern era of crisis intervention has existed since the mid-1940s. It was expanded from the early work of Erich Lindemann (1944) in his studies of grieving individuals conducted in the aftermath of a major nightclub fire, which proved to be foundational to current crisis intervention concepts. The military writings of Kardiner and Spiegel (1947) defined the three basic principles of crisis work upon which crisis intervention is grounded: immediacy of interventions; proximity to the occurrence of the event; and the expectation that the victim will regain homeostasis and return to an adequate level of functioning. Crisis intervention has proved to be an effective frontline helping model for victims of diverse negative life situations, especially critical incidents that present extreme stressors and may result in psychological trauma (Everly, Flannery, & Mitchell, 2000; Everly & Mitchell, 1999).

There are critical factors that must be assessed by caregivers in order to provide appropriate levels of care for survivors. Every individual is a part of a larger system and there are many factors that play a critical role in posttrauma recovery. While there may be many models of crisis intervention and many ways in which caregivers can help survivors, there are key principles that must be considered within any intervention. While survivors generally experience common short-term reactions, they do not always experience long-term negative psychological and emotional outcomes. On the contrary, the research points to high levels of resiliency within the human spirit and a great capacity to experience significant levels of posttrauma growth and development.

"Call Me if I Can Help"

The first church I (Kevin) ever pastored was in an inner-city mission in Cincinnati, Ohio. If I asked a question, it was highly likely that someone would actually answer back. I learned on some points not to ask a question because I really didn't actually want an answer—for example, "Is the person next to you the devil?"

Most of us are not good at asking for help or receiving help from others. This statement can be interpreted as dismissive and appear to be a false attempt at caring. It is very similar to one of the most common Western greetings, "How are you doing," (a statement), not "How are you doing?" (a real question) as we walk on past with absolutely no attempt to hear the answer. This greeting is actually often a statement, a greeting with no consideration that someone would actually take ten minutes to convey the deep anguish of his or her soul.

"Call me if I can help." This well-intentioned but ineffective phrase is perhaps one of the most frequent things said to survivors. People say this for a number of reasons. First, when someone is hurting or in crisis, we feel as if we should say something to them. Second, we often really do feel compelled to help the person.

Third, we sometimes say this knowing that he or she probably will not call us, which allows us to safely extend the offer while going on with our lives: "You know, I told her three times to call me if I could help her, but she never once called." Caring platitudes are as ineffective as spiritual platitudes.

"Call me if I can help" is not a statement that is hurtful, unlike some things people say. However, it is rare that the person actually will pick up the phone and ask for help. It really does depend a lot on how people say it and the actions and words that surround the event. Survivors often do not want to impose their own suffering on the busy lives of others.

So you may wonder, what is a more effective way to come along-side the hurting? When Karen's husband died suddenly in an accident, leaving her with two young children, several women from her small group showed up at her house immediately. Being moms, they quickly assessed the practical daily needs and provided care. Later, Karen stated that for several weeks she had walked around in a posttrauma fog and had little recollection of what had happened. She recalled that she had absolutely no idea who had done what, but amazingly, the dishes were done, the girls were taken to school, the laundry was washed and put up. When asked what had helped her the most, she immediately pointed to the practical care of her friends.

Taking the time to assess a need and meeting it is one of the most critical things that caregivers can do in the aftermath of a critical incident. There is perhaps no organization or group more positioned to provide this practical care then the church. During the first 48 hours following a critical incident, survivors normally have a diminished capacity to function. Assessing a need and meeting it provides an important ministry. What if the good Samaritan had rushed by the man on the side of the road, saying, "Bless you, my son, be warm and fed and heal quickly" as he went on to his destination? The Bible addresses this in James 2:14-17 as viewing our faith and actions as inseparable. "What good is it, my brothers, if a man claims to have faith but has no deeds? Can such faith save him? Suppose a brother or sister is without clothes and daily food. If one of you says to him, 'Go, I wish you well; keep warm and well fed,' but does nothing about his physical needs, what good is it? In the same way, faith by itself, if it is not accompanied by action, is dead" (NIV).

Do No Harm: Make Sure Your Actions Are Helpful

The Samaritan stopped and met the need as he was able to do in the immediate aftermath, which sustained the life of the victim. It is important to make sure that your actions are actually helpful. One survivor talked openly about how the well-intentioned actions of her family had made things much worse for her and had hindered her recovery after the death of her husband of many years. While she was out of the house, her children had come into the house and had removed all of his clothing. They felt that this would be difficult for her to do and that her failure to take any action toward disposing of his things was hindering her recovery. Unfortunately this is not an isolated event. Other survivors tell similar stories, such as the couple whose baby was delivered still-born and whose family and friends take all the things from the nursery before she comes home from the hospital. These attempts to shield a person from the pain may actually compromise the grieving process and can have long-term adverse impacts on an individual's recovery.

Learn to ask. Obviously, some tasks are a given and close friends can do simple tasks without risk; for example, the trash can be emptied and the dishes washed and put up. However, perhaps the wife doesn't want her deceased husband's clothing to be washed because it is the last remaining thing that she has that smells like him. One grieving father kept the dirty clothing of his dead children for a lengthy period of time in an airtight bag. Sometimes he would open the bag and hold the clothing to feel a connection with his children. That old neglected fishing pole that hasn't been used for years or the coffee mug with the missing handle may be of special value to the survivors. Don't assume that you know what is best for them. Everyone processes trauma and loss in a different way. To ask permission is helpful for example, saying, "Jenny, would it be helpful for me to take Bobby to school this week for you?" Maybe Jenny will be grateful, but perhaps she needs that routine, a very important daily ritual for both of them to maintain a special connection with her son. Perhaps it would be more helpful if you picked him up after school or went shopping for the groceries. Maybe she would rather you stay with the kids for a few hours while she gets away to shop and clear her mind.

There is a big difference in saying, "Call me if I can help" and, "What is one thing that I can do for you right now that would be most helpful?" Sometimes, in the immediate aftermath of a loss or traumatic event, survivors may not be able to think clearly enough to assess what they need. They may forget to do the basic things such as eat, drink, pick up the kids from school, and bathe the children. Asking if you can do a basic task can often be what is most important to a survivor. In doing these humble acts of service, you provide a practical ministry of presence that is comforting, and yet the survivor does not feel the need to entertain you while you are trying to help. One often sees this at a funeral. The primary griever sometimes has little opportunity to mourn at the funeral because he or she is so busy taking care of everyone else there. While this may be a healthy adaptive coping strategy for some, other survivors may greatly appreciate someone to play hostess to others while they at times need to slip off to be alone.

Coordinating Assistance

One of the things that survivors often say was the most helpful to them in the early aftermath was the behind-the-scenes coordination that someone did to take care of the basics of life that still needed to be addressed. In times of crisis people often feel compelled to provide help, but they don't know what to do or if they should even offer. One of the things that is most helpful in getting survivors through the early aftermath is to have a trusted friend who can assist them with the details. There are a number of things that can be coordinated that can be immensely helpful.

Taking messages: Sometimes in the early aftermath the phone rings constantly. This outpouring of support can be very helpful and can make the survivor feel loved and cared for, and yet it can also be an emotional drain and keep them from being able to concentrate on completing critical tasks associated with the traumatic incident. One survivor found her church to be very helpful after the sudden death of her husband. Several of June's closest friends took turns coming to her house and answering her phone and door for her. They kept a journal of supportive phone messages, giving a quick summary for her to read later. They would also record and prioritize calls of offers for help and business issues, and would then talk with the survivor to help her figure out how to handle these things so she wouldn't need to do it alone.

Incident-focused peer support: It is very helpful to have someone come along beside you who has experienced something similar and has survived it. What they learned from their experiences can be very helpful as long as they are objective and emotionally healed enough to be able to help. One of June's friends, whose husband had died a few years earlier, went with her to the funeral home to make arrangements. Her knowledge of the process was a great help to June. Unfortunately, in the immediate aftermath of a crisis event, you are forced to make decisions when you are at your worst mentally and emotionally. It is easy to make poor decisions when the decisions are emotionally based because you are so cognitively impaired. Churches should assess their congregations and identify individuals who are willing to provide companioning in times of crisis. These specialized ministries may include support for divorce, job loss, grief, terminal illness, murder, suicide, death of a child, or traumatic accident. This will be discussed further in chapter 6.

Coordination of services: Assigning a trusted friend to help coordinate logistical needs is critically important. This may include coordination of people who want to bring meals, take care of the children, do the laundry, fuel the car, and pick up family from the airport. It is very common for survivors to go about life in a daze for a few days to a few weeks following the traumatic event. They often desperately need the help of others during this time. We often underestimate how important these simple acts of service are for the affected person, both emotionally and psychologically. When people give the gift of service they provide a huge ministry to survivors that is often what is remembered most in the long term.

Stabilize the Situation

One of the basic principles of crisis intervention is establishing safety and stabilization of the situation. The following are the kinds of things the caregiver can do to provide safety and a stabilizing element (Ellers, 2008).

- Assess and provide for basic survival needs and comfort (e.g., liquids, food, shelter, clothing, heating/cooling).
- Help survivors achieve restful and restorative sleep.
- Preserve an interpersonal safety zone protecting basic personal space (e.g., privacy, quiet, personal effects).
- Provide nonintrusive, ordinary social contact (e.g., a "sounding board," appropriate uses of humor, small talk about current events, silent presence).
- Address immediate physical health problems or exacerbations of prior illnesses.
- Assist in locating and verifying the personal safety of separated loved ones/friends.
- Help survivors take practical steps to stabilize and resolve immediate problems caused by the disaster.
- In times of chaos and trauma, a person may feel very alone even though he or she is surrounded by people. As panic and anxiety can be contagious, the caregiver can serve a critical role in bringing stability to affected individuals and groups.

Hear the Story (Normalize, Validate, Ventilate)

"Normalizing the situation" refers to acknowledging and facilitating understanding of the trauma, as well as providing an opportunity for the survivor to express thoughts and feelings about it. The caregiver tries to create a sense of normalcy that contrasts with the abnormal disaster situation. In addition, the caregiver can:

- Facilitate resumption of normal family, community, school, and work roles.
- Help survivors reduce problematic tension, anxiety, or despondency to manageable levels.
- Support survivors' indigenous helpers through consultation and training about common stress reactions and management techniques.
- Remember that to do effective pastoral care you don't always have to talk about the crisis, disaster, pathology, stressors, emotions, theology, grief, or loss. Sometimes, the emotional and spiritual caregiver may provide an

opportunity to talk about things in the context of pre-disaster living or other things of interest to the person. Sometimes, giving people permission to focus on something other than the stress of the disaster is helpful.

- Also, helping people resume family routines is important. This is especially important for children and the mentally ill, who find safety and security in the routines of life. Encourage people to take a break from the disaster scene when possible. Some disaster relief efforts have facilitated this through hiring clowns, hosting block parties, providing therapy dogs, and so on.

The most important thing is to follow the lead of the survivors. It is common for them to use humor to help them cope with their situation. Sometimes their humor may seem to be inappropriate in the circumstances, but it is their way of coping. Romans 12:15 instructs us to "rejoice with those who rejoice; mourn with those who mourn" (NIV).

Information is a powerful agent in helping disaster survivors regain a sense of normalcy and control of their lives. Thus the pastoral care provider should seek as much knowledge as possible to assist people when in the field. Remember that it is difficult for people to focus on higher levels of processing, such as emotional and spiritual issues, when they are seeking to meet basic needs. Providing handouts about key resources and issues can be helpful and also lend a sense of normalcy.

Preparing Survivors to Cope and Referring Them to Appropriate Care

Interventions must focus on strengths and seek to build resiliency. Survivors often have many coping mechanisms that they can use to face the stressors of a disaster. The caregiver can help a person recognize her or his own assets and resources, as well as facilitate access to resources and people that can help her or him cope. The strengths perspective seeks to identify, use, build, and reinforce the strengths and abilities that people have, in contrast to the pathological perspective, which focuses on their deficiencies and inabilities.

In general, the caregiver can help a person cope by:

- Emphasizing a person's strengths, assets, and resources
- Facilitating access to assistance, social services, family, and social networks
- Assisting survivors in solving immediate concerns
- Helping a person problem solve and take action to address his or her problems
- Helping a person maintain a hopeful and optimistic attitude
- Helping survivors draw on their faith and beliefs, and reconnect with their faith community

While the comfort given by an emotional and spiritual caregiver in the crisis setting may never replace the comfort that comes from close friends and family, he or she plays a critical role in the transitional period. When possible, caregivers should seek to connect people with others. After a critical incident, survivors are immediately concerned with the safety of their loved ones. Providing a mechanism through which survivors can make contact with loved ones is critical. Disaster relief organizations will often try to distribute phone cards to survivors to assist in this endeavor, and relief centers and comfort stations may serve as gathering places for both survivors and relief workers. One positive element of traumatic events is that they may serve to strengthen existing relationships or forge new relationships. As will be discussed later, this is especially important in the early stages following a disaster.

Meeting basic needs in the first 48 hours is an important factor in how survivors fare in the long-term aftermath. It allows them to prioritize their limited cognitive resources toward doing critical tasks and to expend available emotional energy to cope. Meeting basic needs is also grounding. When you feed, clothe, or hydrate someone, it is comforting. These actions meet the basic life-sustaining needs that we all have beginning at infancy. This type of care is not only life-sustaining but emotionally and psychologically important as well. Remember that in the early aftermath, survivors are often cognitively impaired. It is kind of like trying to drive an eight-cylinder car on only four cylinders. It may get you there, but you waste a lot of energy, big hills will be a real challenge, and it will likely take a lot longer.

Quick Reference Tips for Providing Practical Care during the First 48 Hours

- Reach out to survivors; don't expect them to ask you for help.
- Seek to serve.
- Understand that in the first 48 hours survivors may be overwhelmed by the critical incident and need more support, help, and direction than normal. However, make sure you don't do things they can do for themselves and further disempower them by making them feel as if they have less control.
- Assess what would be most helpful to the survivor and don't assume that you know what they need.
- Care provided should meet basic needs and be practical.
- Understand that a compassionate presence may be as helpful as anything else.
- Make sure that you do not do anything that interferes with a survivor's natural coping mechanisms.
- Get permission from the survivor before helping, but see if there are ways that you can help coordinate care within the faith community for immediate and ongoing support.
- When there is an unmet need, find and coordinate a link for them with a referral for support or services.

Think about This

1. If you have experienced a critical incident, what practical care was the most helpful to you?

2. Quickly assess the group to find out what resources exist in the group. What have you experienced in your life that would make you a good caregiver for a particular type of traumatic incident?

3. How well does the church fulfill James 2:15-17?

4. Has the church turned this care over to the government? If so, is this effective and the right thing to do?

CHAPTER SIX
Putting the Pieces Together

Information is empowering and critical to help survivors, in the immediate aftermath of crisis, confront the reality of what has happened, make good decisions, and begin the healing journey. We need accurate facts in order to make decisions about our lives on a daily basis. If you doubt the power of information, just ask anyone who has had a loved one disappear, die, or be murdered in a way that leaves them with unanswered questions.

Even when a crisis or traumatic event does not directly touch our lives, we still crave information. Many Americans regularly stay tuned to network news when a crisis event happens. Viewership of news coverage during and following the events of September 11, 2001 clearly indicated this. We hated what we saw but couldn't seem to tear our eyes away—perhaps if we watched it one more time, it would seem real and we would gain some level of understanding. But often even smaller-scale events generate this type of interest and information seeking. A large percentage of Americans (us included) tuned in to news on a regular basis to see if there were any new developments in the case of missing Florida toddler, Caylee Anthony. We grieved along with millions of Americans when her remains were found near her family's home in Florida. Even though we didn't know her and had never met her or her family, many Americans wanted information about her disappearance and death.

The who, what, when, where, and how can sometimes help us as we grapple with the why. However, the why questions rarely get answered. And answering the why questions is not our job as crisis responders. But crisis responders can help fill in the who, what, when, where, and how blanks. Often, the information that survivors need comes from doctors or medical personnel, law enforcement, or other emergency service personnel. When survivors are distraught, confused, and grieving, they are often not in the best frame of mind or position to seek and find the information they need. Crisis responders can be their advocates. I (Jennifer) have often played the role of advocate and communicator for those in distress. As a responder, I can more calmly and reasonably make requests, ask questions, or even negotiate with medical or law enforcement personnel when survivors are not up to the task of doing this for themselves.

The Importance of Getting Information

You may not fully understand the importance of information until you sit with someone who is desperate for facts. This can be a situation where a loved one is missing and information of their whereabouts or safety is unknown. It can be in the case of violence or murder when a loved one has been killed, but the family does not know who the murderer is or how the murder happened or why. There are so many situations where the lack of information itself creates a crisis.

I (Jennifer) have a dear friend and colleague who lived this experience personally with the murder of his brother. In 1990 David's older brother, Charlie, was murdered. Charlie had been missing for a short time when police discovered his body. David and his family had many questions initially, and David acknowledges that they were more fortunate than most families in that they were able to get much information about Charlie's death. David is from North Carolina but was living in Oregon at the time his brother was murdered. He immediately flew home when he got the news. "The next day, my nephew and I went directly to the sheriff's office. We needed to know everything," David said. David acknowledges that he and his family were very fortunate that law enforcement had a lot of information about Charlie's murder, and they shared all the information they had with the family. They were caring, compassionate, and understanding. David says he was able to reconstruct everything that happened the night his brother was murdered and that getting this information was extremely helpful in the grieving process. Charlie's body had been dumped in a local river and was discovered weeks later. "If they had not found a body, our journey would have been much different," David acknowledged. David's father identified Charlie's body—a difficult task but a necessary one. Some family members did not want to see the body, as it was badly decomposed by the time it was discovered. But seeing the photos of his brother's body was very important to David, as was walking through everything that happened to his brother the night of the murder, including visiting the property where the murder took place and the bridge where Charlie's body was dumped into the river. Some people, like David, need as many facts as possible. Others will want limited information. This is where it is critically important to ask individuals in crisis what information is important to them and then to respect their needs and wishes.

Not everyone is as fortunate as David's family who received needed information. One man I (Kevin) was working with following the death of his only son had a very different experience. Cliff received a frantic call from his teenage daughter. She had gone to her brother's house, but he did not answer the door. Peeking in the window, she saw that he had hanged himself. As Cliff and his wife rushed to the scene, they struggled to make sense of it. They were totally unprepared for this. Their son had recently lost his job because of a change in ownership of his company, and this had rocked his world. He had never made any prior suicide attempts, nor had he given any indication that he wanted to die. Their minds raced as they arrived at the scene—was it suicide or a murder? Both would be difficult to handle, but suicide seemed more complex and harder to accept.

They sat for hours outside the police perimeter, unable to enter the house. Cliff had tried to enter the area but had been told that if he entered, he would be arrested. The pain was immense for the family, and they had no information other than that their only son was dead. Cliff said that, while he knew that during the investigation it was impossible, all he wanted to do was to go hold the body of his dead son in his arms. But this was denied him, and he would not get the opportunity to get close to his son that day. The police provided no information to the family during the investigation, and Cliff reported that there wasn't even an acknowledgment that there was family waiting outside the police tape. They sat for hours waiting for any information at all that would help them begin to make sense of it. The only interaction that they received was what they observed among the law enforcement personnel on scene, who to them seemed to be "cavalier and uncaring." As the police began wrapping up the investigation and prepared to leave the scene, Cliff expected that someone would talk with them, but responders only took the body of their son away and everyone started to leave the scene. One of the police officers walking by suggested that the family might want to board the door up as someone might come in and steal their loved one's belongings. They waited for someone to approach them with some information, but that did not happen. As the police got in the car to leave the scene, Cliff ran to the squad car, knocked on the window, and asked for information. The officer, who seemed to be disturbed by him, rolled the window down a few inches, then flipped a card to him with a phone number and said that he could call the number for some information.

As I sat with Cliff several years after, the wounds from the uncaring police scene that day still stung. He vividly recalled entering the house with his wife and daughter and feeling absolutely alone, abandoned, and lost about what to do. During the weeks and months that followed, he found little support anywhere in the community. Out of the pain of his experience, he began to talk to crisis intervention teams and others to educate them about how to help families in the aftermath of trauma and loss. He recalled that any form of information or even an "ounce of compassion would have gone a long way" to help his family recover from their loss and grief.

Why We Avoid Survivors: Trauma Changes Us

Survivors may feel avoided by professionals, and they may also feel that family members are avoiding them. Emergency services personnel deal with trauma every day, and if they are going to be able to continue to do their job year after year, they have to find a way to manage the trauma that they experience. They must learn to separate their emotions from their capacity to do their job. There are many ways they learn to do this. Sometimes, these are healthy but other times they are unhealthy and emergency personnel can take their stress out on others, including family, friends, or themselves. Unhealthy options can destroy them. However, there are many other wonderful helpers who have found ways to build a protective barrier around themselves while at the same time being able to reach out to survivors in a caring and compassionate way. As crisis responders, we are also at risk and must carefully guard ourselves to make sure that we don't become callous and indifferent while at the same time not becoming traumatized or burned out.

As a well-seasoned crisis responder for a number of years, I (Kevin) have seen many horrible things. It does change you. I have a very different view of death as a result. I tend to live more in the moment and to enjoy my interactions with my family and friends more intensely than before. However, every time I take leave of someone I love, I am very aware that we must hold life loosely and that this may be the last time that I ever see him or her again. I don't fear death. I may fear the process of dying a painful death, but I do not fear death itself. I can say this now, having looked death in the face on at least two occasions.

How You Can Help

One thing that crisis responders can do is help persons gain access to information and to dispense information as it becomes available. Learn to be an advocate for survivors to help them get the information they need so that they can begin to put their lives back together. On a crisis scene, emergency responders have a variety of tasks to complete, which takes concentration. In order to do this, they become adept, in most circumstances, at shutting off their emotions and concentrating on what they need to do. It is important to allow them to do this, otherwise the investigation will be colored by personal emotion or, for example, the paramedic may become so emotionally involved that she or he loses objectivity and fails to perform the needed life-saving tasks.

The crisis responder can communicate information between the survivors and professionals in such a way that it can actually protect survivors and be helpful to all parties. This is where a chaplain on scene can play a critical role. This can also involve the filtering of information to make sure that individuals in crisis are not bombarded with rumors, speculation, or inaccuracies. Inaccurate information can actually be quite harmful and can cause secondary trauma. Sometimes people want so desperately to help survivors and to say something that makes them feel better that they will make up information or distort the truth. One of the things we often see is that people will tell only part of the truth.

After Sharon's husband committed suicide, she first told the family that he had died of a heart attack. However, it soon became evident that people were going to find out and this would be even more devastating to her children. A few days later, with the help of a counselor, she sat down with her children and told them the truth. It would have been far more devastating for her children to learn the truth from someone else, and it might have made them lose their trust in her. It is obvious that we must use wisdom to discern when and the amount of information we give.

During the Sago mine disaster in 2006, many of us witnessed the devastation that can come from inaccurate information given to those who are facing a crisis situation. On January 2, 2006, there was an explosion at the Sago coal mine in Sago, West Virginia. The blast and its aftermath trapped thirteen miners for nearly two days. As loved ones of the trapped miners waited for any news of the miners' condition, most were in a very vulnerable state emotionally and psychologically. Television news stations such as CNN, Fox News, and MSNBC covered the event around the clock. This tragedy will be remembered primarily for the misinformation that was given to the public in the aftermath. The media reported that twelve miners had been found alive and that only one person had died. Families rejoiced at the news that most of their loved ones were safe, only to find out a short time later that the information provided by the national media was incorrect. In fact, only one man, Randal McCoy, had survived the blast. The twelve others were dead. The news devastated families, and the misinformation caused additional pain and unnecessary wounding to a time of trauma and tragedy.

Body Identification/Viewing

There may be occasions when you will help prepare a survivor to identify or view the body of a deceased loved one or when you might even choose to or be asked to accompany them in the view-

80

ing. As a chaplain, I (Kevin) have done this many times; and I can think of few tasks more emotionally and physically challenging. Except for those individuals whose job brings them into contact with death on a regular basis (medical personnel, police officers, firefighters, paramedics, and others) for most people, seeing a dead body can be a traumatic experience, even if you are not acquainted with the person. Most often, when body viewing or identification is necessary, it is because there has been a sudden or traumatic death, and the entire process can be quite difficult for survivors.

There is a distinction between identification and viewing. If identification is required, this means there is some doubt about the identity of the deceased person or that the identity needs to be verified. In these cases, someone who knew the deceased person is needed to view and identify the body. This can be very difficult because the body may not be in a good condition, and the viewer may be subjected to uncomfortable and unfamiliar sights and smells.

But even if there is no question regarding identity, survivors will often choose to view the body of a loved one. However, others may feel strongly that they do not wish to see the body. Either choice is valid and should be supported. In many cases, viewing the body of a loved one, particularly following a sudden or traumatic death, can help survivors come to terms with the reality of the death. When we are told that someone has died unexpectedly, the first thing we usually say is "No!" Sometimes, being told that a loved one was killed in an accident is simply not enough. It just doesn't make sense. It takes time to adjust and accept the finality of death. Actually seeing and touching the body is a tangible experience that makes the death real and can help many people start the process of healing. Spending a few final moments with a loved one and "saying goodbye" can be an important part of viewing the body. However, for others, seeing their dead loved one is not helpful.

The family of a young woman who was killed in a tragic and traumatic automobile accident chose not to view the body. Her mother stated that she had a beautiful picture of her daughter in her mind. A picture of her daughter alive, vibrant, and full of life was what she wanted to remember.

Another woman arrived on the scene of a fire that had taken the lives of her adult daughter and son-in-law. She begged to see her daughter, but the firefighters would not allow her to view her daughter because her charred body had been burned beyond recognition. The chaplain talked with the fire chief and convinced him that she really needed to see her daughter. The fire chief talked with the mother, and they came up with a plan to help her meet her need to connect with her daughter. One of the things the chief also needed to do was to protect his firemen from the mother's strong emotions, and he also feared that viewing her daughter's body would further traumatize her. Emergency personnel put the deceased daughter in a body bag and moved her to the ambulance. They covered everything but an unharmed arm and hand. The chaplain sat with the mother while she held her daughter for a few minutes and stroked her hand and cried. After a few minutes she got up, hugged the chaplain and fire chief and said "That was all I needed." Then she left the scene. This woman was able to start her grief journey because she was allowed to mourn the loss of her only daughter in a way that would help her heal. The chief was able to protect his firemen from the mother's emotions. The chaplain played a critical role in helping advocate on behalf of the woman.

Survivors have a strong need for information, and, with the help of an objective advocate, they can often get what they need more easily than if they tried to get it alone. As a crisis responder, it is important to talk through these choices with survivors. They need to weigh the options. While some people will have a strong and immediate sense about what they need to do, others will be torn between a need to view the body and a desire to avoid painful images of their loved one's death. The best gift you can give is to be present with survivors as they make this decision and support the decision they make without judgment. Although you may have concerns about how they will feel about their decision weeks, months, or even years down the road, it is important to validate their feelings. Let them know that you understand how difficult the decision is.

Offer to be with them if they choose to view the body. It is also important to prepare them for what they might see and how they might feel or what they might experience. Allow them to progress at a pace that they can handle. You may first walk to the room and describe what they will see. Ask them if they are ready to go in. Tell them that you are going to step inside and allow them to take a few seconds to prepare themselves. In your role as caregiver, it is important that you adjust yourself to their pace and what they can handle.

It is also important to help families understand that each of them may feel differently and may make different choices about viewing the body. Painful feelings and resentment can often occur within families when different personalities and different grieving styles cause family members to make different decisions about viewing a body or to have different responses. It is important to help families understand that while it might be helpful for one person to view a body, this may not be helpful, and might even be harmful, for another person.

One family faced a difficult situation when one of the daughters-in-law did not want to go to a funeral, even though she really loved and had a close relationship with the deceased. Even though she was in her thirties, she had never been to a funeral and was unsure of how she would handle it. One of her friends stayed with her at the house during the funeral, and another family member took pictures after the funeral in case she wanted to see them later.

Small and Large Group Community Briefings

An effective tool frequently used by crisis response teams is a group briefing. Specific training for this is given is by the International Critical Incident Stress Foundation in their Critical Incident Stress Management (CISM) materials called the Crisis Management Briefing (CMB). The National Organization for Victim Assistance (NOVA) utilizes a similar group crisis model.

Large group meetings are basically, as we say in the South, "y'all come" sessions. These sessions are held for the general public or a large group within a specific organization. People in leadership positions provide key information about the critical incident. These sessions can be helpful to counter rumors that quickly start and spread like wildfire when there is a lack of information. It also brings people together and can provide a safe place for them to congregate and perhaps get some smaller group interaction or one-on-one crisis intervention as well.

Sometimes it may be best to hold information briefings for smaller groups that have been affected in specific ways. One large

Christian organization ran into some difficulty as funds had diminished and the administration determined that there was an immediate need to eliminate and consolidate some positions within the organization. While some of the supervisors may have had an idea that this was coming, most of the general workforce was taken by surprise. There was a general sense of shock as people began losing their jobs. Over the next 48 hours there was a growing sense of apprehension, and the rumors began that there were going to be cuts every few days until it was over. It did not help that the key upper administrators were all out of town when the cuts actually happened and there was a growing sense of fear among the workers. Several of the department heads handled it well and pulled their employees together and gave them as much information as possible. Other departments received very little information, and it caused much more anxiety. Finally, the word got to the administration that they needed to more strategically plan how they could deal with this. Much too late, they held a Crisis Management Briefing (CMB), which made a major difference in the atmosphere of the workplace.

People need information; without it they will fill in the blanks, often with misinformation. Needless to say, humans usually expect the worst, and often we find that our perceptions are worse than reality. In all my (Kevin) years of working with survivors in the aftermath of traumatic events, if I have been honest with them, I have never had anyone tell me that they wish they had not known something. They may wish the event had not happened or wish they could have changed the situation, but they have always wanted and needed to know the truth.

When there is missing information, it is hard for survivors to move on with life. We all know that there will be many things that we will never know. But, be an advocate and be sensitive to survivors so that they can face the truth and begin to put their lives back together.

Reconstructing the Story

Just as survivors need to be able to put pieces of information together, they also need to be able to put the pieces of the story together. Crisis survivors can play a critical role in this. After

Robert's wife and children died in a flash flood accident that suddenly swept their car off the road, he desperately needed to put the pieces together. An important part of his recovery was to go back to the scene of the accident and walk the path where his family members had died. Sometimes, well-meaning people want to protect survivors from the trauma because they feel it will interfere with their healing. However, we commonly find that survivors may not be able to adequately mourn their loss and may get stuck in their grief until they are able to confront certain things and deal with the traumatic elements. As a chaplain, I have many times accompanied people back to the scene of a crime, accident, or death. As horrible as it may sound, some family members may feel a need to try to experience what happened in the last hours of their loved one's death. One of the things that we have found is that if people don't know something or if there is a missing piece, they will usually make up something to fill in that blank space. There have been many times when I have worked with a surviving family in the aftermath of an accident, and after viewing the body of their loved one, they have said that they pictured it being much worse than it actually was. Obviously, each situation must be carefully assessed, because some situations are unbelievably horrific.

When we try to cover up the truth, we often find that survivors sense that they are not getting the whole story, which may evoke a picture in their minds that is even worse than the actual reality. Sometimes it takes a little while before survivors can truly grasp the situation. After Hurricane Katrina, I (Kevin) was coordinating crisis care chaplains for the DMORT team at the morgue at a temporary site outside New Orleans. At first, our chaplains worked inside with the DMORT staff and went outside to minister to survivor families who came to the gate to get information. There was one man who would show up at the gate every few days wanting to know if anyone had found his mother. As the weeks progressed, he became more frustrated with the lack of news. There were hundreds of bodies in the morgue, and it involved a lengthy process for the DMORT team to identify many of them. One day the man came to the gate and demanded that he get some information. I went out to talk with him. He said, "Chaplain, just let me go in there. I have known my mother for fifty years, and no one would know her better than me. I don't mind, I just need to know. Let me go look!" I sat him down, and we had a frank talk. I explained that there were hundreds of bodies in the morgue and described the process the team had to go through first. He understood that part. So I continued. I explained how the bodies were coming to the morgue and that they were sometimes so decomposed and bloated from lying in the heat and water that without trained medical personnel one couldn't even tell the sex, age, or race of the person. He got quiet and then said, "Thank you, Chaplain." We talked for a while, and he went on his way. As difficult as this information was for him to hear, he needed to hear it.

It is difficult to tell people difficult things, and yet hiding the truth when they want it is rarely helpful. Sometimes our own insecurities keep us from doing this. We can't bring ourselves to give the horrific news, so people continue searching. This is not to say that you need to tell every single detail; that is not necessary. However, we find that it is important not to lie when asked about something. Sometimes, as caregivers, we will have information that we are not able to give because it is not our place to give it or because the investigation is still underway. In these situations, you can simply say that they are still doing the investigation and then try to ensure that the authorized person provides the information at the appropriate time.

Information about victims must be given with compassion and sensitivity. Sometimes professionals who work where there is a lot of death and trauma develop a protective veneer that seems cold and uncaring to survivors. One woman told the crisis response team after a bad experience with the hospital staff, "I know they didn't know my mother and her death didn't mean a lot to them. But it did to me. Even if they didn't care, couldn't they at least act like they cared?"

Quick Reference Tips for Providing Information during the First 48 Hours

- Help survivors gather the critical facts about what happened.
- Advocate for survivors to get adequate information.
- Understand that survivors may express strong emotions and that those with the information may not want to be

exposed to this and may need a liaison to help convey the information.

- Ensure the amount of detail given is age appropriate.
- Information should be provided in a timely manner.
- Information should be given sensitively, with care and compassion.
- Information should be given in a language the person can understand.
- Remember that in a state of crisis survivors often have diminished short-term memory capacities.
- Try to surround survivors with a solid support system when they have to confront difficult information.

Think about This

1. If you have experienced a critical incident, what information did you need the most?

2. What information helped or hindered your recovery process?

3. What resources are currently available in your church to help facilitate the flow of information for survivor families and church members in a time of crisis?

CHAPTER SEVEN

Educating Survivors about the Past, Present, and Future

In times of crisis, people often function in a reduced capacity. One of the things that we, as crisis responders, give survivors is the gift of education. There is an old saying, "Advice is like garlic, a little bit goes a long way." When it comes to times of crisis, if we understand what is happening to us and are equipped to help ourselves, we feel less afraid. The last chapter dealt with the importance of providing survivors with information about the details surrounding the critical incident. In this chapter, we will focus on how we can provide education to empower survivors to cope with a crisis. When crisis responders give individuals and families a basic education on posttraumatic stress—the causes and symptoms, as well as provide some fundamental tips for self-care—we give a tremendous gift. I (Jennifer) took my first class in CISM (Critical Incident Stress Management) from a skilled counselor and crisis responder named Bob VandePol. I must credit him with the following description, which made so much sense to me that I have continued to use it throughout my years as a trainer in the field.

Imagine you have never had a cold or flu virus—have never heard about it or received any information or education about it, don't understand the symptoms or what causes it. Let's say that in the imaginary world where you have never had a cold or flu virus, you come home from work one snowy winter day feeling a bit tired and somewhat unwell. You can't put your finger on what's wrong, but you just don't feel like yourself. As the evening progresses, you feel worse. Your throat begins to feel scratchy, and you feel tired and achy all over. You go to bed early in the hope that a good night's sleep is all you need to feel normal again. However, when you wake up in the morning, you have a pounding headache. Your scratchy throat has become painfully sore and raw. Your nose is so congested that you can barely breathe, and the aches have gotten worse. You begin to panic. Since you have never experienced symptoms like this and have never heard about them, you are certain that something terrible is happening to you. The fear and anxiety about your symptoms might add to your stress, further compromising your immune system and actually making you feel worse. Because you are worried about the symptoms, you visit your doctor. After asking you some questions and doing some basic tests, he tells you he thinks he knows what is wrong. He asks if you have a sore throat and a stuffy nose, and if perhaps you have had a headache and some muscle aches. As he lists the symptoms, you are thinking, "Yes, yes—that is exactly what I feel." You feel that he understands what you are talking about. He would then tell you that you are having a normal human experience. As we go through life, when we are exposed to certain viruses, our body's immune system reacts to kill the invading virus. The consequences of our body's natural immune response fighting off the virus is certain symptoms such as a stuffy and runny nose, sneezing, coughing, sore throat, headache, and sometimes fever and muscle aches and pains. He also reassures you that viruses are frequent, common, and generally not dangerous. He explains that the immune systems of most healthy adults fight off the average cold or flu virus quite easily. He tells you that all of the symptoms you are experiencing seem normal to him and he is confident that within a day or two you will start to feel better and that within a week or two at the most you will be fully recovered and have no more symptoms of the virus. He also tells you that while there is no immediate cure he can give you to make your symptoms go away, there are many things you can do to make yourself feel better and to alleviate the degree of your symptoms. These very basic things might even help your body fight off the virus more quickly and expedite your recovery. He tells you to go home and get plenty of rest. Don't do anything too strenuous and get plenty of sleep. He tells you it might be a good idea to eat some healthy food like chicken soup and get some vitamin C by drinking orange juice. He tells you that hot tea with honey and lemon might soothe your sore throat and that over-the-counter decongestants may help your stuffy nose, and pain relievers will help with the aches and pains. By the time you say good-bye to your doctor, you are already feeling better. It helps just to know that what you have is normal and that you will be just fine.

The experience I've just described can be very similar to what people experience following a crisis or trauma. Posttraumatic stress is a normal reaction to an abnormal event. God designed our minds and bodies with a "response system" to crisis and trauma just as God created an immune system to fight off infection and disease in our physical bodies. However, prior to experiencing a traumatic event, most of us have no idea what it feels like to have this posttraumatic stress alarm system go off in our minds and bodies. These symptoms can be frightening. Many people describe feeling as if they are going crazy. When you experience these things, even though they may be normal, they don't feel normal. However, when a crisis responder is able to explain that these frightening symptoms are normal and are our mind's and body's ways of responding to what has happened, the intense fears decrease.

A very important point that is often missed in our managed care system of health care, however, is that people need to be heard. Sometimes when we say, "You are experiencing a normal reaction to an abnormal event," this can sound clinical and dismissive. It doesn't feel normal to them, and they want you to understand that it is scary. It is critical that we understand that we often need to first take time to hear and validate the symptoms, allowing survivors to give voice to their fears before we try to provide education.

So, as crisis responders, we have two primary responsibilities in crisis education: symptom education and care information. The first is to explain and normalize the symptoms of posttraumatic stress. In the early hours, before many of the symptoms have set in, it can be helpful to tell survivors what they might expect to experience. You might also give them a handout of common symptoms of posttraumatic stress. Remember, those who have just experienced a critical incident are not thinking clearly and may not remember the symptoms you describe. Having something in writing to refer to can be helpful a few hours or a few days later.

It is also incredibly helpful to give them some basic and practical information about caring for themselves in the aftermath of the crisis. Many crisis responders try to make this step far too complicated. We are not asking you to practice psychology, therapy, counseling, or medicine. In fact, you should refer any potential medical or mental health issues right away. But what you can and should offer is good, basic advice. Yes, these are things most people have probably heard before. In fact, your mother or grandmother probably gave you most of this advice at one time or another. But during a time of crisis, most people need clear and simple directions for helping themselves. Nothing is too simple. People need to be reminded of the importance of basic physical necessities like eating and sleeping. It is normal for both appetite and sleep to be disturbed during a time of crisis, so people have to be intentional about getting rest and eating. Eating well—protein, whole grains, fruits, and vegetables—is very important. Try to help people understand that overeating or not eating will only exacerbate their symptoms. Most people will have difficulty sleeping, so they might need tips on healthy and productive ways to get better sleep. But even more important can be giving them recommendations on what *not* to do. Often, the first instinct people have is to self-medicate the anxiety they are feeling with drugs or alcohol. Many think alcohol will calm them down and help them sleep. While alcohol does initially act as a depressant, after a few hours in the system it becomes an irritant and can disturb sleep. This is also a very dangerous time to use any mood-altering substance. Individuals who would normally not be at particular risk for dependency may be much more likely to develop a dependency on alcohol or prescription drugs at this time.

Dispensing Information

When I (Kevin) bought my first house, I was excited about new home ownership. However, the people who had owned the house before me had either not known how to take care of the yard or had neglected to do so. Either way, it was in great need of attention. Being a novice gardener, I began looking around at the lush yards that adjoined mine with great envy. I would see the owners out on the weekends with their little green spreaders putting things on their yards and watering. Being a busy guy with many ideas about fixing the house to my standards meant that I had a lot of things to do and not a lot of time. Seeing my lawn with the sparse grass and full of weeds bothered me, so I headed to the nearest garden store. I didn't bother asking for any advice; I just looked for the bag of fertilizer that seemed to guarantee the quickest results and the greenest grass. Seeing that the yard had been neglected and was far behind the other yards, I decided that it probably needed some more nutrients, so I increased the dose a little. It was late spring and, sure enough, we were blessed with a rainstorm that conveniently followed my efforts; within a few days the grass was noticeably greener. Encouraged by the results of this fantastic product, I headed back to the garden store. After all, my yard still had a long way to go to catch up with the other yards, and being the great, benevolent dispenser of fertilizer that I was, I intended to bestow even more fertilizer as an extra blessing. This time I put another batch of the fertilizer on the yard, which now had more than doubled the amount recommended. Unfortunately, it didn't rain this time, and for several days the sun beat mercilessly on my yard. Water costs money and it was a lot of work to drag the water hose across the yard, so the lawn went many days without water. My benevolence, though well intended, was not greatly appreciated by the grass, which was severely burned by the overfertilizing and started turning brown.

Sometimes we, as crisis responders, although well-intentioned, can fail to assess what survivors need and so fail to give the right information, give information in a way that is not able to be absorbed or retained, or give too much of a good thing. How do we educate survivors in a way that will help them in their posttrauma and loss recovery?

Educating about the Impact of the Past

When I (Kevin) was working my way through seminary, I worked with several older ladies in the central distribution section of a hospital. I was one of the few men working in the department, and because I had no seniority and was a part-time employee, I got stuck with whatever job no one else wanted to do. One of the tasks we had to do was to fold the surgical towels that were to be sterilized in preparation for surgery. While we folded towels, the women would tell many stories about their families and particularly about their husbands. One story has always stuck in my mind, and I have used this as an illustration many times when working with trauma survivors. One of the women loved to go fishing; she and her husband would go fishing, and sometimes she would cook the fish and bring it to the office to share with me. For years, they spent time fishing off the shore, but finally they had saved enough money to buy a fishing boat. It was one of the models of bass boats that sat very low in the water. Her husband would rarely let her drive the boat, but one day after launching the boat in the water, because the dock was full, he allowed her to drive it away from the dock as he parked the truck and boat trailer. He gave her strict instructions to stay by the dock, but this was her chance. She decided to take it out for a quick spin. She felt a rush as she accelerated the boat out of the "hole," as it is called, and got the boat up on plane as she skimmed across the top of the water. As she rushed to get back to the dock before her husband returned to meet her, she neared the buoys indicating a "no wake zone." She realized that she was making a huge wake, and fearful of getting a ticket, she suddenly shut the throttle completely down. However, she did not consider the other consequence of throttling down, and the huge wake she had created suddenly caught up with her from behind, overflowing the boat and submerging it! Needless to say, her husband was not a happy camper, and they had a very difficult time getting the boat back out of the water and now faced an expensive long-term project to fix the damage.

We've already discussed the importance of making an assessment and of hearing the survivor's story. These two things are important in crisis intervention because they help confirm the reality of what the survivor has experienced. We often hear, "She is doing so well. I can't believe how well she is doing." Whenever we hear this, as crisis responders we encourage people to check back with them. I often tell people that they will find that survivors will fluctuate broadly in how they are doing. I also point out that "doing well" is a perception, and it should not be anticipated that survivors will always be "doing well." Crying and feeling emotionally low is to be expected as well and is a normal part of the recovery process. Too often in the church we expect people to put on their face and act as if all is well when they really want to tell you that life sucks, but they don't feel they can. As crisis interveners, we need to help survivors understand how the things they experience can affect them in the future. Sometimes, in our counseling practices, we find people coming in with presenting problems that in reality have very little to do with their current situation other than the fact that it is a trigger from unresolved trauma and loss from their past. Sometimes in the aftermath of a traumatic incident, survivors will fill their lives with nonstop activity. While this self-protective activity can help distract them from their pain, they can't run from things forever. Survivors have different needs in terms of how they look at the realities of the past. The research is clear that not everyone needs to spend a lot of time talking about traumatic incidents of the past. However, people do need to understand and prepare for the possibility that, like the woman in the boat in the story above, the emotional wave of the incident may hit them long after they expect it to, and with devastating results, if they are not prepared.

In the first year after a couple's college-age daughter was murdered, they engaged in nonstop activity to help change the law in order to protect young women from stalkers. In an interview several years later, they said that the magnitude of their grief did not even hit until about a year later. They had busied themselves so much that they had suppressed their grief as much as they could and did not allow themselves to mourn. Their activities had a positive result in that it allowed them to channel their energies into making a difference in the face of something so horrible. However, looking back, they realized that they held their grief internally through that year and so experienced many negative physical symptoms that they did not recognize until later were the result of their internalized grief. When we provided them with information about the impact of trauma and loss, they were amazed at the symptoms they saw in themselves and said that it would have been very helpful to have known that these were normal signs and symptoms of stress. They said, as have so many others, "We thought we were going crazy," which further added to their stress levels. What the couple found was that their symptoms continued to build to the point that they became almost nonfunctioning in the aftermath. Helping survivors understand the potential for a delayed impact from trauma is critical.

Educating to Protect Survivors from Others

It may sound harsh to talk about how others may prey on survivors in the aftermath of trauma and loss, but this does happen. As crisis interveners we have seen many examples where survivors have been the victims of theft, shady business deals, and attacks on character. Sometimes the abuse is blatant and intentional; however, most of the time we find that survivors are hurt by others unintentionally. Regardless, this secondary wounding can be extremely hurtful and sometimes even more harmful than the critical incident itself. When Lee's father committed suicide, Lee, as the oldest son, went to the house to help his mother. When he was in the bathroom cleaning the blood from the walls of the bathtub where his father had shot himself, he heard his parents' pastor in the other room talking. The pastor told Lee's mother that his father was a bad man and had gone to hell for his actions. Lee reports that when he heard this he saw a flash of red before his eyes, and it was all his wife could do to keep Lee from throwing the pastor out the window.

Unfortunately, this is not an isolated incident; we hear story after story of similar comments that people make in the aftermath of critical incidents. They go something like this, "Well, she really hadn't been in church recently, and I knew something was going to happen." "Didn't you guys know that he was suicidal?" "I'm so sorry about your rape, what were you wearing?" Granted, sometimes traumatic events happen as a result of poor choices. But even so, to rub that in the face of a survivor is never helpful and to sit in a self-righteous place of judgment is not what Jesus taught us. Sadly, where we often hear these statements of judgment within the walls of the church. These comments often arise from our insecurities. People who make these statements try to rationalize to make themselves feel more secure, which may lead them to the belief that surely if something bad happened, it must be the result of sin or bad choices. Therefore, it won't happen to them. Ironically, because we all struggle and fall far short of the glory of God, we are all deserving of judgment.

In the Old Testament, Job struggled with this with his so-called helpers. As we often say, "With friends like that, who needs enemies?" We find this in the story of the man who was born blind from birth in John 9:1-3. The disciples ask Jesus, "Who sinned," this man or his parents? The church has to teach a solid theology of suffering that will help people survive when they are in the midst of a storm. When I (Kevin) was doing interviews for a trauma video series, I did some in one particular church where there had been a number of traumatic incidents. I was struck by how the solid theological teachings of this church had been so positively embedded within the lives of the people who had survived these horrific incidents. Although these individuals struggled, questioned, and experienced their individualized crises of faith at times, they all held fast to the theological concept that had been taught in the church relating to the sovereignty of God. These survivors held onto this idea as their theological rock when their world seemed to be spinning out of orbit, and it really served as an anchor in their storms.

When asked, "What was the most helpful thing anyone did to help you get through the death of your husband?" one woman immediately referred to something her pastor had done. In the immediate aftermath, her pastor sat with her and told her about how his dad had died when he was younger. He told her that people often said things that were hurtful and that she should be prepared for this possibility and should understand that they really didn't mean to hurt her, they just didn't know what else to say. She talked about how this made a huge difference to her when people did say something hurtful and how it helped her to not take it personally.

Educating to Cope with the Present

Remember that in the first 48 hours following a critical incident, the crisis intervention and the primary focus is not on the past or future, but on coping with the present. The primary goal of the crisis intervener is to help stabilize and protect survivors and help them cope with things while they are functioning at reduced capacity.

When Donna's thirty-four-year-old husband was killed suddenly in a work accident, she was almost totally immobilized. As expected, she struggled with the reality that he had died and experienced difficulty even providing for the basic needs of herself and her surviving two daughters. The pastor called the church counselor to see what the counselor could do to help. Being a trained crisis intervener, he quickly assessed her level of functioning. He asked her for the names of two of her most trusted friends living nearby. He asked if he could call them to assist her. When he called, they came immediately to the house to provide comfort and assistance. Prior to leaving Donna's house, he provided a brief crisis education to Donna and her friends and explained some of the common symptoms that she and her daughters might experience. He also assessed what Donna's friends could do to help her in practical ways. With Donna's permission, each of them took different tasks, coordinating their efforts. When the counselor met with Donna and her friends later, they all three talked about how helpful that brief education had been. It enabled them to better anticipate reactions and needs and to create a plan for best coming alongside her. Sometimes a mistake that we make is to try to give too much education to survivors when they don't have the cognitive functioning level to process it or the memory to retain it. Thus, often your best bet is to educate those who will provide ongoing support. There is a lot of available literature on how to help people in times of crisis. You can leave this literature as a handout to serve as a guide.

Educating for What to Expect in the Future

As mentioned earlier, in crisis intervention during the first 48 hours, the primary focus is on coping in the present. However, we need to help protect survivors from making poor choices that can have a very negative impact in the future. Major life decisions should not be made in the early aftermath of a critical incident. By addressing during the first 48 hours some of the common symptoms that survivors may experience, caregivers can pave the way for future dialogue and for follow-up care later on as survivors begin to fully experience the magnitude of their loss. It is important to educate family and friends about how to help survivors in the future. One of the most common comments that we as crisis care responders hear from survivors is that the care tapers off, and after a while they feel abandoned. Their support system often diminishes about the time they need it the most.

One of the important tasks is to help families regain a new sense of normal and to stabilize the family by helping them return to as much of the old routine as possible. This is important for children who look to their parents to show them how they should handle these new stressors. Sometimes in the aftermath of a crisis there is a strong sense of vulnerability, and some families may be fearful of allowing family members to be apart. While this is okay in the immediate aftermath, crisis responders need to help families navigate this new terrain and build a new life. In our grief interviews, we have had many people grieve the fact that in the death of a loved one, someone else emotionally died and abandoned the others who were still living. In one of the grief interviews we were doing for a crisis response series, a teenage daughter angrily confronted her mother, saying that just because her sister had died didn't mean that she had too. She went on to say that she needed a mother, and even though she too was grieving the loss of her sister, she was also grieving the fact that she was emotionally and physically losing her mother as well. This was very eye-opening for her mother.

Quick Reference Tips for Providing Education during the First 48 Hours

- Make sure you really listen as survivors tell you the symptoms that they are experiencing as well as any fears and anxieties that they may be having as a result.
- Remember that "normal" posttrauma symptoms do not feel normal to survivors.
- The primary focus of crisis education in the first 48 hours is on stabilizing, protecting, and meeting basic needs.
- Remember that in times of crisis a survivor will often have an impaired level of cognitive functioning as well as a diminished capacity to retain information in their short-term memory. Thus, any information given should be simple and direct.
- Information should be shared with trusted friends and family who will be supportive and monitor the care of the survivor.

99

Think about This

1. Is there a difference between advice and education? If so, what?

2. What do you think needs to precede advice and information giving by caregivers?

3. How well has your church prepared people for dealing with crisis?

4. Can you think of a situation in which a person did not get good advice or information in a time of crisis and there were negative consequences?

CHAPTER EIGHT

Telling the Story

The Importance of Telling the Story

It is important for survivors to have an opportunity to tell their story. In chapter 6 we discussed why it is important to help survivors get the information they need so they can create their story. When something horrible happens in our lives, we have a need for someone else to bear witness to what we have experienced. When my (Kevin's) daughter, Mallory, was a little girl, she used to love putting puzzles together. She would come into the room with her puzzle box and in her cute little three-year old voice say, "Daddy, you pway puzzles wif me?" Standing in front of me, she would dump her box upside down and giggle as the puzzle pieces tumbled out all over the floor, creating a mess. As the pieces randomly scattered around the floor and under the furniture, the fragments had little resemblance to the picture on the front of the puzzle box.

Mallory and I had a way of dealing with this mess. The usual routine was that we would both sit down on the floor, in the mess that had been created, and work on it together with the expectation that together we would work at it until the mess began to take shape into something recognizable. There was order in the way we approached the puzzle. First, we would turn all the pieces over so we could see the front of each piece. Then, we would begin to search for the outside edges and create the border and start sorting the pieces into categories as to where we thought they fit. It was a lot easier to put the puzzle together if you had something to look at. The bigger and more complex the puzzle mess, the longer it took to put one puzzle together.

It was always more fun to do with someone else who also liked to do puzzles. When I was not there, she would try to recruit her sisters to help her. Their interest was not really in helping her, and their attention would wander, which would frustrate her. Sometimes Mallory would have a piece of puzzle in her hand which hovered over the right area, but because it was oriented wrong, it wouldn't fit. I would then put my hand on hers and turn the piece so that it fit into place. I always enjoyed the look of satisfaction on her face when it suddenly made sense to her. On a few occasions we would get almost done, but a few pieces were missing. We would search under all the furniture until we found the missing pieces. Sometimes there were pieces that someone had lost in the past, and there was always a sense of incompleteness when this happened. We even glued several of her favorite puzzles to a piece of cardboard, so they could be mounted and she could enjoy the finished picture.

Mallory's puzzle-solving process has many similarities to the way we, as crisis responders, come alongside survivors in times of crisis. We can help them figure out their messed-up life that may seem to lie shattered into a million pieces. In the aftermath of a critical incident, survivors may emotionally regurgitate their trauma story to you. As they talk, their story, much like the pieces of a dumped puzzle, tumbles out and spews everywhere. It isn't pretty or organized, and it may not make much sense. However, as you enter their world and are there with your psychological catcher's mitt, you can help them contain the chaos. As you sit with them in the midst of their emotional mess, you establish borders of safety; and as you listen, you help them sort out the mess so they can begin to put their life back together.

We often hear survivors talk about how it seems that their life was shattered, and in the acute aftermath of a critical incident, this is true. By your presence you can play a powerful role in helping them put their life back together and bring back safety and order as they rebuild. While they may wrestle with big questions, they rarely want your answers. Learn to sit and walk with them in their recovery journey at the pace they set. Together you will figure it out.

There is something that happens as people tell their story: it begins to make more sense to them. The story is somehow held between you, so that they begin to see the picture more clearly. You are helping them make it real. You are confirming that yes, you have experienced this and yes, it is overwhelming and painful. You listen, give objective feedback, summarize, ask clarifying questions, and listen some more. All these things really help.

One of the first things that survivors need to come to grips with is the reality of what has happened. As they tell their story, you can help them do this. In the acute aftermath the traumatic event often seems unbelievable, and they will often swing between denial and the reality of the situation. They need your patience and your love through this process as you help them face a new reality.

"Do You Want to Talk about It?"

How do we get survivors to talk about what is going on inside them? We frequently hear people say to survivors, "Let me know if you ever need to talk" or "Do you want to talk about it?" These are often unnecessary questions that sometimes actually inhibit survivors from talking. There are far more effective ways of getting people to open up and talk about what is bothering them. Finding someone who can truly hear your pain, who is a good listener, is a rare gift within our society.

A few years ago, I (Kevin) was sitting in yet another boring committee meeting. I had been tasked with the responsibility of taking minutes for the meeting, but I was having continual problems with my computer. About every ten minutes, my computer would lock up, and I would have to shut it off and start it up again. I mentioned my frustration with the "stupid computer" to the guy next to me several times, but his computer was working fine and he made no comment. As the hours wore on, my frustration began to rise. If the window had been open, I would have been tempted to "accidentally" drop the computer out of it. However, as fate would have it, the window was securely locked. When we took a break, I stepped out into the hallway. My mobile phone rang, and it was one of my coworkers from the office with a work-related question for me. As we were talking, she asked how things were going. I told her that all was well with the meeting, but I was about ready to throw my computer out the window. I will never forget her words. She said, "Oh my goodness, you have had so many problems with that stupid computer over the past few months, haven't you?" Finally someone had heard my lament and understood. An amazing thing happened then. Instantly, I felt my frustration begin to dissipate, and within a few minutes of talking with her my stress and frustration was almost gone. While I would have liked my computer to be fixed, it wasn't going to happen that day. However, someone had taken the time to simply hear my frustration, validate it, and walk where I walked. She said that she had once had a computer with similar problems, and it had been a huge source of frustration to her too. If she had said, "Do you want to talk about how frustrated this makes you feel?" I would have probably felt like telling her to jump out the window and take the computer with her.

People in crisis don't want to be viewed as clinical projects and often negatively react to clinical phraseology or jargon. One night while working as a chaplain, I (Kevin) received a call to work with the family of a woman had been brought into the emergency room. The family had been sent to a small waiting area to wait for news, and they were highly anxious. Another chaplain intern had gone in on the previous shift but had almost gotten punched in the face by her brother and then had been kicked out of the room. The ER staff was not sure how receptive the family would be to me but felt they needed someone to be with them. A man had broken into the patient's house at night. Hearing a noise, she had left her bedroom, taking a machete with her to see what the noise was. She discovered the intruder, who took the machete from her and followed her through the house slashing at her. Her brother had come to the house and followed the trail of blood to his sister's room, where he found her. When the brother had told the intern chaplain the story, the chaplain said to the brother, "And how did that make you feel?" He said, "How the [bleep] do you think that made me feel?" and shut down. Perhaps the awkwardness of hearing about that level of trauma had made the intern chaplain fumble for words. So he fell back into the classic TV sitcom question that epitomizes mental health intervention. When I sat down with the brother later, I simply listened as he told me about how angry he was at the chaplain. When I validated his anger, he went on to talk about the feelings of rage he had at the man who had done this to his sister.

People are more open to talking with you about things if you are a good listener and actively engage them. Use simple reflective statements as you tune into their pain to help them open up. However, you should never try to force people to talk about something until they are ready. Different people process things in different ways and with different timing.

In the immediate aftermath some survivors want to talk, and their story and pain just gush out. For others, it may take a while before they feel the need to talk. Forcing someone to talk about something before they are ready may be counterproductive to their recovery process. When you meet people at the level where they are and you hear and validate what they are feeling, they are more likely to go deeper. People often subconsciously put out feelers to test if you are a good listener and a safe person. If you miss their cues, they may not go any deeper. One of my favorite kid movies is *Shrek*. In the movie, Shrek is talking with Donkey and says, "Ogres are like onions." Donkey doesn't like Shrek's self description and wants to argue with Shrek and change his analogy to something more pleasant, such as a cake or parfait. Shrek gets annoyed with Donkey for presssuring him to change his analogy and is adamant that ogres are like onions.

People are like onions because they have layers. Not only that, their pain has layers too. Often as the layers beneath the protective skin are exposed, tears and raw emotion begin to flow. It is for this reason that we often do not want to allow anyone to get beneath that protective layer that we portray to the world. To open ourselves to others is to be vulnerable. Many people have deep pain at the core of their being that they have learned to protect by adding layers to hide the insecurity and deep wounds and scars of the soul. If you provide a safe and trustworthy environment and are a good listener, it is likely that people are going to talk to you. However, not all people need to talk. Some may find it more healing and therapeutic to engage in shared activity or to express their emotions through art, dance, or journaling.

We have always found it interesting to watch the transformation that often occurs in some of our counseling clients. As they begin to deal with inner issues of self-worth, become more confident, and gain a healthier view of their bodies, they often begin to wear different types of clothing. Women, especially, who have been deeply

wounded sexually, will sometimes wear oversized, ill-fitting clothing. This subconscious behavior is often an attempt to hide their
body and their deep wounds. For them, clothing serves as a protective barrier to the outer world.

What is most critical is that the survivor be able to acknowledge
what has happened. As a survivor tells his or her story, the story
becomes real, which allows the survivor to gain perspective and to
acknowledge that, "Yes, this really did happen to me." It is important to have others acknowledge the event and to bear witness to
the survivor's pain.

One survivor tells a story of how she was falling apart during the
last hours of her father's life. Her father was in a coma, and the hospital staff had not been very helpful. She didn't feel that anyone
around her, including her family, was being very helpful. She
finally slipped away to the restroom, where she locked herself in a
stall. As she sat there sobbing, she heard another woman come into
the restroom. As hard as she tried to contain her tears, little sobs
still came out. Soon a dainty, lace-trimmed handkerchief was
passed under the stall by an unknown lady, who said, "Are you all
right? Can I help?" Her story just poured out as this unknown and
unseen caregiver attentively listened to her. The woman gave her
some words of comfort, prayed with her, and slipped out the door.
The survivor later recalled that she never knew the woman's name,
never saw her face, and could not remember much of what she had
said to her. However, this angel of mercy provided just what was
needed through a powerful ministry of presence as she bore witness to her pain.

Jesus found it important to process the events that he and his followers experienced in ministry. In Mark 6:30-32 we find an example
of Jesus and his disciples needing to refuel physically and emotionally by getting away from the crowd. When the crowd would not
leave them alone, they went away in a boat to have some privacy.
Talking to God and to others is important. God has designed us to
be in relationship with others; we were not created to be alone. In
the beautiful Garden of Eden, we find Adam as a newly created
being among the animals and wonder of nature. God looked at all
that God had created and said, "It is not good that the man should
be alone" (Genesis 2:18 KJV). Although God was with Adam, God
designed humanity to be in relationship with other people.

How Can We Help Survivors Tell Their Story?

There are several things that are helpful in meeting the needs of survivors and in enabling them to be able to tell their story.

Establish a Safe Environment

Establishing a safe environment is critical in order for survivors to feel comfortable telling their story. First, there cannot be any sense of judgment. Unfortunately, the church is not always the safest place to share your deepest hurts. When there is an environment in a congregation in which a person feels as though he or she must act in a certain way, survivors can be hindered from expressing how they truly feel. In the early aftermath of a traumatic event, survivors often have a range of raw emotions that are not always rational and may appear to be contrary to how the survivor "usually" or is "supposed" to act.

You will often find some bad theological concepts spewing from the mouths of survivors in the aftermath of trauma and loss. The church must be there, but this is not the time for a theology lesson. Usually survivors will correct this with time. How caregivers respond to this raw emotion is important and can have a long-term impact on how survivors will relate to others and how safe they feel about opening up in the future.

Second, a safe environment respects confidentiality. Survivors need to know that what they express is private. It is important to talk about this and to explain the bounds of confidentiality.

Third, it is also important for caregivers to come to where the survivor is and create a physically comfortable space. For example, if survivors are sitting, sit with them. Don't sit behind a desk, because it creates a barrier. People often talk best when they are doing the normal activities of life. Disaster chaplains understand this and will often provide emotional and spiritual care while helping survivors clean up or carry groceries to the car, for example. It can sometimes be important to get away to a safe place. While it may be more threatening to the caregiver to meet at the person's home instead of at the church office, it can be important in helping the person feel comfortable. As a police and fire chaplain, I (Kevin) have found it important to meet with police officers and fire fighters where they feel most comfortable. For law enforcement personnel, this is often their patrol car. Doing a ride-along with the officers, where you can be with them in their world, is often an excellent opportunity. When I worked at a children's shelter, I rarely sat in chairs in a therapy office to talk with the kids. I took them outside to the basketball court, walked around the pond, or sat on the floor and played a game with them. After establishing rapport and a safe environment with them, the kids were much more open to talking.

Fourth, sometimes we tend to move too quickly to talk about what has happened and how survivors are doing. Taking time to get to know them and relate on less emotionally laden topics can serve you well in the long run. Letting people talk cognitively about the details of the event or how it has impacted others is often a good step toward their opening up about how they are dealing with things. I often ask how their family, friends, or others are coping. After this, I may reflect that the situation must be difficult for them as well. Sometimes a simple reflection of things that you have heard them talk about is far more effective in encouraging them to open up than is coming out and asking, "How are you doing?"

Allow Them to Talk When They Are Ready

It is important that you don't try to force survivors to talk about things. Sometimes they get tired of well-meaning people asking, "How are you doing?" Survivors sometimes report that they may be asked this dozens of times within a short period. Being available is critical. Often people may not be ready or may be unable to talk about things at one point, but when you stop by a little later, they are more than ready. Unfortunately, often the time when survivors really need to process things may come weeks or months later after people have stopped asking about it.

Survivors Vary in How Much They Need to Talk about It

As human beings, we are all different, and one of the ways in which people vary widely is the amount of time and the degree to which they need to process things externally. Much of this need derives from our personality type preferences and whether we tend to be more extroverted or introverted. There is an old saying in counseling that I have heard for years, "If you are around an extrovert and you don't know something, you haven't listened. If you are around an introvert and you don't know something, you haven't asked." There is a broad range where people fit on the introversion and extroversion scale, and yet we all fit somewhere on the spectrum. Extroverts tend to process things more in the outer world and generally have more of a need to process and refuel by being with others. A few weeks ago I was checking out at Home Depot, and the cashier, within the few minutes of my being there, had told me that she had gone through a divorce, was going back to school, liked to cook, and a number of other things. I left the store laughing at how open she was to share what was going on in her world with a total stranger. She continued this running dialogue with everyone through the line. Introverts, on the other hand, tend to live more in the inner world and have less need to process and refuel with others. For some people, an experience hasn't really happened if they haven't shared it with someone else. For others, the experience is private and they have absolutely no need to tell others. For example, when crisis response team members returned from working at the World Trade Center site after the 9/11 attacks, some of the team members attended all the group processing opportunities, accepted invitations from churches to speak, talked to the media, and met with family and friends extensively. Others came back and needed several weeks before they wanted to talk at all, and then these people only talked about their experiences minimally.

It is also important to consider your own preference for processing, because it will greatly influence how you feel others need to process things. As human beings we generally think that we have the right perspective on life. If we like to receive gifts, we will probably like to give gifts. If we feel like crying is helpful, then we tend to think that crying is helpful for others. There is an old saying that states, "Advice is like garlic; a little bit goes a long way." Explore more than you direct or give advice.

Remember that there are many ways, other than talking, that people find helpful for processing their thoughts, feelings, and experiences. They may find an outlet in music, drawing, painting, exercise, worship, sports, or other activities. The key is to help survivors identify what would help them most to process their experience and not assume that you know what they should do.

All people have their own unique style of coping. The key is to explore with survivors to make sure that they have a support system available and understand their options.

Use Effective Active Listening Skills

Make sure that you are emotionally present with the survivor. Make sure that your nonverbal language indicates that you want to be there. Sit with an open posture, lean forward, make eye contact, use reflective statements, and paraphrase and summarize what you hear them say. One of the most common mistakes we make as caregivers is failing to keep our own mouths shut and talking more than the survivor. Pay attention to how much you are talking. Sometimes I have caregivers count their words to measure how much they are talking. In times of crisis, caregivers often become nervous and feel a need to fill silence with words. This can significantly interfere with the survivor's natural coping mechanisms, because it signals your anxiety. Understand that in the early aftermath, survivors aren't going to hear much of what you say and have a significantly reduced mental capacity to process information.

Learn to Ask Great Questions

Learn to ask leading questions. An effectively asked question can communicate that you are listening and can elicit more information, clarify, and summarize. When survivors talk about their experiences, it often comes from the heart. When you are able to contain this for them, you hold their story in a way that they can see it a little more clearly. You help them paint a picture of what has happened. As time goes on, this picture will be ever changing for the rest of their life, as they see things a little differently in light of more information, a revised worldview, and new experiences. But don't ask so many questions that you bombard the survivors. Again this reflects your anxiety, not theirs.

Barriers to Good Listening

There are many things that can serve as barriers as you seek to be a good listener and it is vital for you to be aware of several things as you spend time with people in pain. Take time to assess the following.

Am I Feeling Present with Them?

Have you tuned out all the distractions in your own life to fully and completely concentrate on the survivor? If by nature you tend to be easily distracted, try to reduce your stimuli by facing toward a quiet area or getting away from other people. Turn off your cell phone. Nothing is more distracting than your phone going off at a pivotal moment in the conversation. Before meeting with the survivor, take a few moments to center yourself through prayer and meditation, and ask God to help you focus on him or her. Too often we rush from one thing immediately to trying to come alongside someone in a meaningful way without ever taking the time to appropriately transition. Make sure that you do not arrive with your agenda to save them but rather to come alongside them and be with them wherever they are.

What Is Going on Inside of Me?

In the heat of the moment, we may miss this important piece of self-awareness. We do not act in isolation when working with others, and things from their experience or story may easily trigger some of our own strong internal reactions. These reactions may be strong emotions from your own experiences of trauma and loss and may take you off on another track of thinking. Either of these has potential to keep you from being present with the person. If you find this happening, it may be appropriate to address it. For example, you might say, "As you were talking, you may have noticed that I had tears in my eyes. That is because my dad died a few years ago and this triggers my grief as well." A simple acknowledgment or self-disclosure can be important in building rapport and connecting with others. Be very careful to limit your self-disclosure. Regardless of how strongly you believe that your experience mirrors theirs, you can never know exactly how they feel. Too often people say, "I know how you feel." You don't. Every person's journey, reactions, emotions, and thoughts are different, and this type of statement can discount their feelings and may shut them down. You also need to be careful to make sure that what you say doesn't change the focus from them to you. A survivor may sometimes feel like he or she ends up taking care of those who are supposed to be taking care of them.

Am I Really Tuned In?

The last travel trailer I (Kevin) owned had a radio installed with a poor antenna. Sometimes there was an annoying sound of static or even an intermittent intruding signal from another radio station. I would sometimes get so frustrated that I would just turn it off, because it strongly distracted from the program I was listening to. This is analogous to us as caregivers when we are not tuned in to those we are trying to help. Have you ever tried to talk with someone who was not tuned in to you?

We live in a world that embraces the "skill" of multitasking. I (Kevin) recently had dinner with some colleagues. As some of us lingered over dinner, one of the women commented about a person who had just left, "Does he ever really have dinner with anyone?" As we looked at her, she explained that he had spent most of the meal tied to his phone, taking calls or text messaging. He never really tuned in to anyone or really listened.

Multitasking does not serve you well when you minister to others in times of crisis. It is something that I (Kevin) really have to work on. I can't truly focus on a survivor and be thinking about washing my car when I get home. I can't adequately concentrate on other things when I am doing crisis response. I have to consciously focus on letting everything else go and tune in to whomever I am working with, or they will not feel heard.

Children are especially sensitive about whether they are being heard. For them it is especially important that you look at them as they talk. I (Kevin) remember that when my girls were little, as I was reading the paper, they would try to talk to me. I remember a conversation with Madison; it went something like this, "Dad." "Yes, sweetie," I would reply as I continued to read my paper. "Dad," the little voice would say again with a little more emotion. "What," I would reply again with my head buried in the paper. "DAD!" I would then look at her. It was only when she could see my eyes that she perceived that I could hear her message. In all actuality, she was right. Survivors need you to be focused and tuned in to what is going on within them. If you are not focused, centered, and calm inside, this will be observed by survivors because their senses are heightened in the acute aftermath of a critical incident.

Quick Reference Tips for Telling the Story during the First 48 Hours

- Seek to be a great listener.
- Learn to ask gentle, leading questions and listen more than you talk.
- Understand that it is important to establish a connection and a safe environment before survivors may be ready to talk about their situation.
- Be available to talk when survivors need to talk.
- Be prepared for strong emotions that survivors may need to express, but don't assume that the absence of this is an indicator of negative coping.
- Remember that survivors may say a lot of things from an emotional place when they are working through their trauma and loss that they don't really believe.
- Be accepting and nonjudgmental.
- Understand that there is a broad diversity in the amount that people need to talk about their situation.
- Balance talking about the critical incident with normal conversation.
- Understand that a survivor's story relating to a critical incident is likely to continue to change as his or her perspective changes throughout life.

Think about This

1. If you were in crisis, who would you want to talk with about it? Why that person?
2. What are some barriers to talking effectively to survivors in times of crisis?
3. Would you rather talk to a stranger or to a close friend? Why?
4. How do you know that you are being heard?

CHAPTER NINE

Hope in Times of Crisis

For I know the thoughts that I think toward you, says the LORD, thoughts of peace and not of evil, to give you a future and a hope. —Jeremiah 29:11

Hope in a future? In times of trauma and loss sometimes survivors may see very little hope in a future. In the face of incredible loss it may literally seem as if life is not worth living, and it may seem as though their future has been ripped away. When Sharon's husband committed suicide by carbon monoxide poisoning in the garage of their home, life as she knew it ended forever. In the early aftermath of her loss, she compared her life to a glass that had been hurled to the floor, shattering into a million pieces. Grief so consumed her that she lost all desire to live. A caregiver from a local crisis response team came alongside her and quickly assessed her suicidal ideations and surrounded her with loving caregivers. Sharon later reported that the quick assessment and protective measures had likely saved her life. The caregiver coordinated concrete helping actions with family and friends, who took turns staying with her and caring for her children, assisting her with the necessary funeral arrangements. However, one of the things that Sharon later identified as being key to her finding hope in her darkest hour was that her caregivers helped her understand how desperately her children needed her as their mother. She said it was only when she looked into the eyes of her children that she discovered she needed to remain alive and secure a future for them.

The Nature of Hope

We believe that one of the most critical factors in determining an individual's long-term recovery from a crisis or trauma is whether he or she is able to access hope. Hope gives individuals the strength to face immeasurable suffering and unthinkable circumstances. Hope is one of the critical things that we look for when assessing the risk factors with a person who is suicidal. Without hope, there is little motivation to persevere through suffering and pain. When all a person can see is a life of suffering and loneliness, life may seem pointless. Remember that in times of trauma, loss, and crisis, people often lose perspective and fail to see the whole picture. Even little things that they could usually weather without difficulty can seem like huge storms that block the face of hope.

I (Kevin) never cease to be amazed at the difference between what the world looks like under cloud cover and from 30,000 feet far above the clouds. Even when I leave the house on a miserable, rainy day, every time the plane climbs above the clouds, the sun shines brightly. It doesn't matter how dark it is on the ground, the sun always shines; always! I rarely think about it. Sometimes it seems that after a few days of clouds, I almost forget how the warmth of the sun feels. If only we could convey this to those who are in crisis.

Helping People Discover Hope

The first thing crisis responders must understand is that the hope individuals need within the first 48 hours following crisis may be fundamentally different from the hope they need for long-term recovery. As we discussed in the chapter on safety, it is critical to find resources that will assist individuals in surviving the onslaught of pain and emotional destruction they will experience in the early hours and days following tragedy. They must find their reason for living in the immediate aftermath of trauma. Within the first 48 hours it may be difficult for them to see a long-term hope and a positive outcome.

Many of the first instincts people have for offering hope may not be effective within the first 48 hours following crisis. We hear many well-meaning Christians offer scripture or theological or philosophical platitudes that they want to be words of hope and comfort. Most of the time they revolve around the theme that everything will turn out OK. While there is truth in scripture such as Romans 8:28, "And we know that all things work together for good to those who love God, to those who are the called according to His purpose," it may not be the truth that individuals in the immediate aftermath of crisis and trauma are ready to hear. Often these attempts to be helpful come across as simplistic clichés that fail to connect with the deep pain those survivors are experiencing.

One of the most well-meaning but ineffective ways we try to instill hope is through lecture or telling people what they should do. We say things like, "You need to think about your children." "Just think about the people who are worse off than you." "You just need to read your Bible and pray more, because as a Christian you should have hope." While these may hold merit, they often have the opposite effect of what we are trying to accomplish. Remember that in the immediate aftermath of a critical incident, a survivor's cognitive capacity may be diminished, so appealing to the rational mind is rarely effective.

One of the best ways to extend hope is to *be* hope. By this we mean that you must believe, to the depth of your soul, that God is good, just, and merciful. And that God can and will heal all the hurts and traumas God's children experience. While you do not need to discuss these convictions with survivors, you must believe them yourself. If we can emphasize one critical element of effective crisis intervention, it is to have a solid theology of suffering. Those who have worked out a theology of suffering will be able to offer the "ministry of presence" more effectively than those who have not.

But theology is always a work in progress, and it will need to be rethought in light of your continued experience. Both us have found that if you minister to people, you will eventually come up against something that has the potential to rock your spiritual world. I (Kevin) have worked as a chaplain in many venues and have seen suffering in the face of injustice and other things that could shake even the strongest Christian. I have found that survivors in the midst of great pain and chaos don't need perfect and unshaken caregivers who have never doubted. These self-proclaimed people of unshakable faith get on my nerves, and I usually find that anyone with too neat a theological package has never really suffered. There is something that I often find refreshing in being around those whom Henri Nowen refers to as the wounded healers. Some of the most compassionate caregivers are those who have walked through the fires of hell and have come out on the other side bruised and battered, singed and stinky, tired, and often shaken, but also refined and victorious.

The Lament of Job

You will find that a survivor's hopeful perspective can fluctuate broadly in the aftermath. It is critical that the church provide an accepting and supportive environment where survivors can use lament to safely vacillate within the painful growth experience. Job is a prime example of a person moving between hopelessness and hope.

Job's Highs and Lows	
Low Side of Job's Suffering	High Side of Job's Suffering
No hope in life "Why did I not die at birth?" (3:11)	Hope in the justice of God "God is wise in heart and mighty in strength." (9:4)
No hope in self "How can a man be righteous before God?" (9:2)	Hope in the mercy of God "Your hands have made me and fashioned me, / An intricate unity; / Yet You would destroy me." (10:8)
No hope in friends "Will you contend for God?" (13:8)	Hope in the friendship of God "Though He slay me, yet will I trust Him." (13:15)
No hope in death "If a man dies, shall he live again?" (14:14)	Hope in the Life of God "If a man dies, shall he live again?" 14:14
No hope in God "How long will you torment my soul?" (19:2)	Hope in God "I know that my Redeemer lives." (19:25)

We see Job's vacillating thoughts and emotions as he progresses from trauma to placing his hope in God. McKenna (1987) states: "Out of the greatest struggles with the contradictions of human existence, faith makes its greatest gains. Faith grows on faith; faith grows out of struggle; faith grows a step at a time" (p. 84).

Drawing Hope from Those Who Have Walked before Us

One of the things that survivors identify as helpful is meeting people who have been through similar circumstances and have come out okay on the other side. We often find that caregivers have absolutely no idea how much hope and strength survivors drew from their simple presence until long after the event. This is where the church can play a powerful role. A few months ago I (Kevin) decided to take the Bright Angel Trail from the top of the south rim of the Grand Canyon to the end of the trail overlooking the great Colorado River. While I expected the trip back to the top to be difficult, I hadn't planned well and I had no idea how exhausted my legs would be after walking nonstop. Highly motivated by the quickly sinking sun and the fact that absolutely no one was around me or behind me as the evening drew near, I quickened my pace. About halfway up the side of the canyon, my legs began to cramp and I was so exhausted that I didn't think I could make it. As I sat down by a pile of rocks, I drew great strength from the realization that it was a marker made by people who also had made this journey. There were thousands of small rocks that people had placed there. As I looked around me, I saw no stack of bones, so I figured that the others must have made it to the top. I added my rock to the pile and struggled on. Remember, survivors don't want perfect caregivers with perfect theologies, they want real people. When you connect survivors with other healthy survivors, you offer hope.

As Christians, we have scriptures that give us hope. In Hebrews 11:1 we read, "Now faith is being sure of what we hope for and certain of what we do not see" (NIV). The biblical writer then goes on to create an extensive picture of many fellow sufferers from whom we can draw hope. He describes a "great cloud of witnesses" urging us forward.

> Therefore, since we are surrounded by such a great cloud of witnesses, let us throw off everything that hinders and the sin that so easily entangles, and let us run with perseverance the race marked out for us. Let us fix our eyes on Jesus, the author and perfecter of our faith, who for the joy set before him endured the cross, scorning its shame, and sat down at the right hand of the throne of God. Consider him who endured such opposition from sinful men, so that you will not grow weary and lose heart. (Hebrews 12:1-3 NIV)

This passage was comforting to me as my (Kevin's) father was dying of cancer. I was teaching an intensive one-week crisis intervention course at a retreat for a number of Orthodox priests who were forming a national crisis response team. Many of them were biblical scholars, and we would sit up late at night talking. One night I was talking about my father's impending death; I said that one of the things that I would miss about him after he died was his prayers because he had always been a great prayer warrior and I had valued his prayers throughout my entire life. Almost in unison, they all looked at me with questioning eyes, as if they were confused by my statement. One of them said simply, "He will pray for you on the other side as well" and quoted Hebrews 12:1. I had always known that I would see him again in heaven and took great comfort in this, but this was a new theological perspective that my church had never taught and I immediately felt flooded with comfort by the thoughts of my father joining this great crowd of witnesses and continuing to intercede for me following his promotion to another world.

Hope in the Face of Death

It was a cold, gray, and lifeless winter day as family and friends huddled together at the graveside as if to glean a small amount of warmth from those shivering next to them. However, the pervasive sense of desolation seemed as bitter as the frigid wind on their faces. "Dust to dust, ashes to ashes . . ." The minister had done his best to identify with them, but the deceased was a stranger. The service was over, but no one moved. Not even the winter air could drive them back to their warm cars. It was as if their blank expressions mirrored that of their loved one in the coffin. As I (Kevin) looked at the mourners, I saw no signs of hope. Although they had created a memorable funeral service, it was evident that there was little to celebrate. I hate these funerals!

As I walked back to my car, I couldn't help remembering the funeral I had attended a few months ago, when I had returned home in great spirits. An old saint of the church who had dedicated her entire life to God had died. This funeral was entirely different. It had been a worshipful celebration of life. Few people had shown up in black, and the surviving family had dressed in celebration colors that indicated a zest for life that honored their beloved. There was hope that their loved one was free of suffering and was now in the arms of her Savior. There were tears, tears of sorrow, yet also full of hope. Those within The Salvation Army call this a "Promotion to Glory."

Key Scriptures on Hope

Here are some helpful scriptures that we find meaningful for survivors.

Matthew 5:1-11 (NIV)

Now when he saw the crowds, he went up on a mountainside and sat down. His disciples came to him, and he began to teach them, saying:
"Blessed are the poor in spirit,
    for theirs is the kingdom of heaven.
Blessed are those who mourn,
    for they will be comforted.
Blessed are the meek,
    for they will inherit the earth.
Blessed are those who hunger and thirst for righteousness,
    for they will be filled.
Blessed are the merciful,
    for they will be shown mercy.
Blessed are the pure in heart,
    for they will see God.
Blessed are the peacemakers,
    for they will be called sons of God.
Blessed are those who are persecuted because of righteousness,
    for theirs is the kingdom of heaven.

"Blessed are you when people insult you, persecute you and falsely say all kinds of evil against you because of me."

Romans 8:18-27 (NIV)

I consider that our present sufferings are not worth comparing with the glory that will be revealed in us. The creation waits in eager expectation for the sons of God to be revealed. For the creation was subjected to frustration, not by its own choice, but by the will of the one who subjected it, in hope that the creation itself will be liberated from its bondage to decay and brought into the glorious freedom of the children of God.

We know that the whole creation has been groaning as in the pains of childbirth right up to the present time. Not only so, but we ourselves, who have the firstfruits of the Spirit, groan inwardly as we wait eagerly for our adoption as sons, the redemption of our bodies. For in this hope we were saved. But hope that is seen is no hope at all. Who hopes for what he already has? But if we hope for what we do not yet have, we wait for it patiently.

In the same way, the Spirit helps us in our weakness. We do not know what we ought to pray for, but the Spirit himself intercedes for us with groans that words cannot express. And he who searches our hearts knows the mind of the Spirit, because the Spirit intercedes for the saints in accordance with God's will.

1 Corinthians 13:7 (NIV)

[Love] always protects, always trusts, always hopes, always perseveres.

Psalm 130:5 (NIV)

I wait for the LORD, my soul waits,
    and in his word I put my hope.

1 Timothy 1:1 (NIV)

Paul, an apostle of Christ Jesus by the command of God our Savior and of Christ Jesus our hope.

Romans 5:1-5 (NIV)

Therefore, since we have been justified through faith, we have peace with God through our Lord Jesus Christ, through whom we have gained access by faith into this grace in which we now stand. And we rejoice in the hope of the glory of God. Not only so, but we also rejoice in our sufferings, because we know that suffering produces perseverance; perseverance, character; and character, hope. And hope does not disappoint us, because God has poured out his love into our hearts by the Holy Spirit, whom he has given us.

Psalm 33:16-22 (NIV)

No king is saved by the size of his army;
    no warrior escapes by his great strength.
A horse is a vain hope for deliverance;
    despite all its great strength it cannot save.
But the eyes of the LORD are on those who fear him,
    on those whose hope is in his unfailing love,
to deliver them from death
    and keep them alive in famine.

We wait in hope for the LORD;
    he is our help and our shield.
In him our hearts rejoice,
    for we trust in his holy name.
May your unfailing love rest upon us, O LORD,
    even as we put our hope in you.

Jeremiah 14:8 (NIV)

O Hope of Israel,
    its Savior in times of distress,
why are you like a stranger in the land,
    like a traveler who stays only a night?

Psalm 131:3 (NIV)

O Israel, put your hope in the LORD
    both now and forevermore.

Psalm 25:3 (NIV)

No one whose hope is in you
    will ever be put to shame,
but they will be put to shame
    who are treacherous without excuse.

2 Corinthians 1:7 (NIV)

And our hope for you is firm, because we know that just as you share in our sufferings, so also you share in our comfort.

Psalm 42:5 (NIV)

Why are you downcast, O my soul?
> Why so disturbed within me?

Put your hope in God,
> for I will yet praise him.

Spiritual Impact of Crisis on Survivors

Hope is a fruit of the Spirit that colors a survivor's relationship with God. However, when people turn from God or the church in times of crisis, it disturbs us. This is especially true when crisis shakes the faith of deeply grounded followers of God. At the same time, crisis may also bring survivors closer to God and their faith community.

As I (Kevin) was working to complete my doctoral project, I logged many hours of videotaped interviews with survivors. Initially, I focused on researching the negative impact that trauma and loss had in survivors' lives. However, as the interviews progressed, I began to see growing evidence that many of the survivors demonstrated indicators of significant posttrauma positive growth. As a result of this awareness, I began to change the format of my interviews with some interesting results. I discovered that sometimes the survivors were aware of the positive changes that they had experienced, but sometimes they were not aware of them until they had the opportunity to tell their story and process it with me. As I began to change the questions that I asked them, I found that the interview process became a therapeutic tool for new understanding and growth for the survivors.

Many people find that they grow more during times of difficulty than they ever do from good times, successes, or mountaintop experiences. Even as we write this book, each of us is experiencing personal difficulties and major life transitions. Yet we can testify to the hope found in our Savior.

Quick Reference Tips for Providing Hope during the First 48 Hours

- Remember that hope in the early aftermath needs to focus on something simple and concrete.

124

- The church can stand as a beacon of hope for survivors when they are unable to find hope in their darkest hours.
- It is better to help survivors discover hope than to lecture them about what they should hope in.
- Understand that it is natural for people to lose hope when life becomes overwhelming.
- Encourage survivors to read the psalms of lament to see that it is okay to struggle with hope.
- Connecting survivors with other survivors who have experienced similar crises and who are emotionally healthy can be helpful.

Think about This

1. What unique perspectives for survivors does Christianity bring to times of crisis and loss?

2. From your experience what are some things people do that can actually serve as barriers in building hope?

3. What has been the most helpful thing caregivers have done to bring hope to you in your times of crisis?

4. Who around you can you think of at this time who may be struggling with hope?

CHAPTER TEN

Caring for People over the Long Haul

Survivors often find that many caring people surround them to offer comfort and practical care in the immediate aftermath of a critical incident. However, one of the most frequent complaints voiced by survivors is that they often feel as though others forget about them soon after the immediate crisis is over. While this book focuses on the immediate aftermath of a critical incident, it is also important to understand that people need care over the long haul for a healthy recovery and to sustain personal growth. There are several frequent themes that we hear from survivors that we will briefly address.

Don't Forget Me

In the early aftermath of a critical incident, people feel compelled to reach out to survivors and generally act in caring and sensitive ways to help them through this difficult time. However, this support is often short-lived. It usually isn't intentional neglect. Sometimes people subconsciously stay away because it triggers their own fears. It may be that they don't know what to say and they are afraid of bringing up the event for fear that it will cause the survivor to feel worse. Often, however, people just get busy with their own lives and forget about the survivors.

Several weeks after Susan's father died, she returned home and plunged back into life. One of her best friends, who had learned about Susan's father's death, called. After about half an hour of Susan listening to her friend's complaining about a minor crisis in her life, her friend said she had to go and hung up without ever asking how Susan was doing since her father's death. Life was back to normal in the larger world, but the reality of Susan's loss was just beginning to become a reality to her, and no one seemed to be interested.

But survivors also forget. One the greatest fears that survivors voice is that they will forget their loved one and the critical incident. Even though it may be painful to remember, sometimes not remembering can be even more painful.

How to Remember

There are many ways that we can help survivors not feel forgotten. Simple questions like the following can open the doors for survivors to talk if they want to and also show them that you remember: "How are you?" "What has changed most for you since your father's death?" "What is the hardest thing for you through all this?" "What is your best memory of your father?"

For those who have lost a loved one, taking time to talk about something especially memorable about the deceased is often appreciated. It is more difficult when the critical incident involves trauma such as rape or incest. However, don't allow the trauma surrounding a death or other critical event to take away from what was important in the relationship or the pretrauma world.

When Jill's daughter announced that she was gay, it shook the world of this conservative religious family who had always strongly opposed this lifestyle. Jill talked about her continuing love for her daughter even though she disagreed with her lifestyle; knowing about it didn't change Jill's love for her. One of the most difficult things for Jill, which she had not anticipated, was how her closest friends and family would react. She recalled that she felt that she was also being blamed for her daughter's lifestyle. "The questions were posed as if I had done something wrong." Not only did people seem to feel the need to pass judgment but some acted as if all that she had had with her daughter through the years was taken away as well. She talked about how her love for her daughter had not changed. When people inquired about her family, they never asked about her daughter. It was as if her daughter had ceased to exist. One of the worst things a caregiver can do is to act as if nothing of significance has happened.

Let Me Have Time to Heal

Survivors need time to heal, but the time frame for accomplishing this will vary among individuals and is influenced by many factors. Too often people look at how a survivor handled a situation in the past and will make an assessment about how they will handle the new situation. This assessment may be totally inaccurate, as each situation brings its own unique challenges and must be assessed in light of not only the past but what is going on in the survivor's present and what might change in the future. Crises must be faced one at a time.

A question that friends and families sometimes ask is, "How long is it going to take for them to get over this?" People often have little tolerance for providing emotional support for survivors over time. Sometimes the sentiment "She just needs to get over it and move on" is publicly voiced; other times it is silently implied.

In our society, people tend to want specific time frames and measurable end points. I (Kevin) hate the word *closure* when talking about grief and trauma recovery. I don't think there really is any such thing as closure. There are certain things that survivors will be able to come to terms with, accept, or understand differently. Many times when people talk about getting closure, they really mean that they want to know that it is over, done, ready to be put away, and then move on. Grief and trauma recovery just don't happen that way. I have found survivors who have boxed up their trauma and put in on a shelf—nice and neat—and tried to ignore it while moving on with life. However, this is often not healthy and may have a long-term negative impact. What has happened must be integrated into the tapestry of the survivor's life. When emotionally healthy people look at their life, they will be able to paint a picture that reflects both the good and the bad and to better understand who they have been, who they are, and who they might be in the future. It is very difficult to deny the reality of what is.

Allowing Time to Heal

To help survivors, you can believe in them and be patient. I (Kevin) remember that when I walked to the bottom of the Grand

Canyon and back up the other side, what had been an enjoyable scenic trip down became an excruciatingly painful journey back to the top. Toward the end, when I looked up at the top, I became discouraged. With each step, the cliff seemed to grow taller. I finally stopped looking to the top and started looking back at how far I had come. This made an amazing difference. Watching the road ahead, I could easily follow the trail; but I would stop when I couldn't walk any further and draw strength from how far I had come. I remember muttering under my breath, "I can do this; look how far I have come."

We need those people who can come alongside us in the dark times of our life, those who can shine a small flashlight on the next step and say, "We can do this together. Let's get you through today." In crisis intervention, the focus is not on the past or on developing a big plan for the future. It is often just focusing on the here and now, sustaining life, surviving the shock of the blast, finding hope for today, and somehow making it through today to tomorrow. While survivors may ask questions in the early aftermath, making sense of the event will be reserved for sometime tomorrow. There will likely be many tomorrows.

I Will Be Different

One of the most frequent things heard from survivors is, "Everyone wants me to go back to being the same person I was before this happened." Life moves on and you grow. Life perspectives may change, but survivors will continue to repaint their trauma story as long as they live. They may become more or less healthy, understand things better, or see life more clearly. But they will build a new life. We often talk about this as a new normal. Many survivors say to their friends, "I will never be the same person." Trauma and loss have a way of changing people, and it is something we should help survivors anticipate. When those in the body of believers walk with survivors through the long-term recovery and help them rebuild their lives, they demonstrate what Jesus intended for the church to do.

A caregiver can help survivors through the dark times of their life by being present with them, a fellow journeyer in their pain. When Jesus left this earth, he sent the Holy Spirit, the Comforter.

130

The one who comes alongside us to walk with us in our pain is our comforter. You can't push or pull people to the place you think they should be in their recovery journey. By listening to their story and talking openly with them, you help survivors come to a realization about what has happened. You can be a sounding board for them, reflecting what they tell you. You can be a mirror for them, helping them see their lives from a new perspective. You can provide the yeast that promotes growth in the midst of the fires of life. You can provide an environment in which they can safely explore all their fears, doubts, and hopes while revising their life assumptions and theological worldviews. The stability within your life can be a lifeline to them when they feel lost. The trauma and loss within your life, from which you have healed, can be an encouragement to them as they desperately seek a beacons of hope, that they are going to make it through today and there can be life tomorrow.

Caring for Survivors from Trauma to Transformation

Wounded caregivers who have healed play a powerful role in walking beside survivors and allowing them to draw on the caregivers for strength. Scripture says much about the power that life's difficulties have to transform us, more closely so that we reflect the image of God. We believe that this transformative growth is meant to happen within the context of relationship. We do not believe that it is possible for a caregiver to have a solid theology and an understanding of suffering if these have not been forged in the furnace of suffering and affliction. No amount of theology, regardless of how accurate, can take the pain from suffering.

When reading the Psalms, we find repeatedly that the psalmists, even in the mist of their pain, chose to trust in the character of a trustworthy and powerful God. God was the source of their hope and recipient of their praise. This is a concept carried into the New Testament as well.

The weight of this is vividly seen in the statement of a wounded Paul, who had been on the frontlines of suffering from many different hardships, as he states:

> Five times I received from the Jews the forty lashes minus one. Three times I was beaten with rods, once I was stoned, three times I was shipwrecked, I spent a night and a day in the open

sea, I have been constantly on the move. I have been in danger from rivers, in danger from bandits, in danger from my own countrymen, in danger from Gentiles; in danger in the city, in danger in the country, in danger at sea; and in danger from false brothers. I have labored and toiled and have often gone without sleep; I have known hunger and thirst and have often gone without food; I have been cold and naked. Besides everything else, I face daily the pressure of my concern for all the churches. (2 Corinthians 11:24-28 NIV)

Despite the intensity of his suffering, Paul could say in 2 Corinthians 4:17, "For our light and momentary troubles are achieving for us an eternal glory that far outweighs them all." This is from a man who suffered far more than most, and yet the suffering he experienced on earth did not outweigh the eternal joy of glory. Many scriptures in the Bible relate to growth and transformation in the midst of life's adverse circumstances.

Passages Relating to Growth and Transformation through Adversity

The following passages serve as a reminder for believers to stand strong and to remember that our current troubles are not wasted moments but have potential to promote growth and development.

Endure hardship with us like a good soldier of Christ Jesus. (2 Timothy 2:3 NIV)

To this you were called, because Christ suffered for you, leaving you an example, that you should follow in his steps. (1 Peter 2:21 NIV)

Therefore, since we have been justified through faith, we have peace with God through our Lord Jesus Christ, through whom we have gained access by faith into this grace in which we now stand. And we rejoice in the hope of the glory of God. Not only so, but we also rejoice in our sufferings, because we know that suffering produces perseverance; perseverance, character; and character, hope. And hope does not disappoint us, because God has poured out his love into our hearts by the Holy Spirit, whom he has given us. (Romans 5:1-5 NIV)

Let us fix our eyes on Jesus, the author and perfecter of our faith, who for the joy set before him endured the cross, scorning its shame, and sat down at the right hand of the throne of God. (Hebrews 12:2 NIV)

But he said to me, "My grace is sufficient for you, for my power is made perfect in weakness." Therefore I will boast all the more gladly about my weaknesses, so that Christ's power may rest on me. (2 Corinthians 12:9 NIV)

But we have this treasure in jars of clay to show that this all-surpassing power is from God and not from us. We are hard pressed on every side, but not crushed; perplexed, but not in despair; persecuted, but not abandoned; struck down, but not destroyed. We always carry around in our body the death of Jesus, so that the life of Jesus may also be revealed in our body. For we who are alive are always being given over to death for Jesus' sake, so that his life may be revealed in our mortal body. So then, death is at work in us, but life is at work in you. (2 Corinthians 4:7-12 NIV)

You hear, O LORD, the desire of the afflicted;
   you encourage them, and you listen to their cry.
(Psalm 10:17 NIV)

Paul quotes Psalm 16:8-11 in Acts 2:

David said about him:
   " 'I saw the Lord always before me.
   Because he is at my right hand,
   I will not be shaken.
Therefore my heart is glad and my tongue rejoices;
   my body also will live in hope,
because you will not abandon me to the grave,
   nor will you let your Holy One see decay.
You have made known to me the paths of life;
   you will fill me with joy in your presence.' " (Acts 2:25-28 NIV)

A miktam of David.

Keep me safe, O God,
   for in you I take refuge.

I said to the LORD, "You are my LORD;
   apart from you I have no good thing."

As for the saints who are in the land,
   they are the glorious ones in whom is all my delight.
The sorrows of those will increase
   who run after other gods.
I will not pour out their libations of blood
   or take up their names on my lips.

LORD, you have assigned me my portion and my cup;
   you have made my lot secure.
The boundary lines have fallen for me in pleasant places;
   surely I have a delightful inheritance.

I will praise the LORD, who counsels me;
   even at night my heart instructs me.
I have set the LORD always before me.
   Because he is at my right hand,
   I will not be shaken.

Therefore my heart is glad and my tongue rejoices;
   my body also will rest secure,
because you will not abandon me to the grave,
   nor will you let your Holy One see decay.

You have made known to me the path of life;
   you will fill me with joy in your presence,
   with eternal pleasures at your right hand. (Psalm 16 NIV)

Who shall separate us from the love of Christ? Shall trouble or hardship or persecution or famine or nakedness or danger or sword? As it is written:

"For your sake we face death all day long;
   we are considered as sheep to be slaughtered."

No, in all these things we are more than conquerors through him who loved us. For I am convinced that neither death nor life, neither angels nor demons, neither the present nor the future, nor any powers, neither height nor depth, nor anything else in all creation, will be able to separate us from the love of God that is in Christ Jesus our Lord." (Romans 8:35-39 NIV)

Consider it pure joy, my brothers, whenever you face trials of many kinds, because you know that the testing of your faith develops perseverance. Perseverance must finish its work so that you may be mature and complete, not lacking anything. (James 1:2-4 NIV)

I consider that our present sufferings are not worth comparing with the glory that will be revealed in us. (Romans 8:18 NIV)

What is more, I consider everything a loss compared to the surpassing greatness of knowing Christ Jesus my Lord, for whose sake I have lost all things. I consider them rubbish, that I may gain Christ. (Philippians 3:8 NIV)

There are strong promises quoted in song from Isaiah 41:10 (NIV):

So do not fear, for I am with you;
    do not be dismayed, for I am your God.
I will strengthen you and help you;
    I will uphold you with my righteous right hand.

Psalm 23:4 (NIV) says:

"Even though I walk / through the valley of the shadow of death, / I will fear no evil, / for you are with me; your rod and your staff, / they comfort me."

God uses your pain to help others, as seen in 2 Corinthians 1:3-7 (NIV):

Praise be to the God and Father of our Lord Jesus Christ, the Father of compassion and the God of all comfort, who comforts us in all our troubles, so that we can comfort those in any trouble with the comfort we ourselves have received from God. For just as the sufferings of Christ flow over into our lives, so also through Christ our comfort overflows. If we are distressed, it is for your comfort and salvation; if we are comforted, it is for your comfort, which produces in you patient endurance of the same sufferings we suffer. And our hope for you is firm, because we know that just as you share in our sufferings, so also you share in our comfort.

God promises that he will never forsake us:

"No one will be able to stand up against you all the days of your life. As I was with Moses, so I will be with you; I will never leave you nor forsake you." (Joshua 1:5 NIV)

The writer of Hebrews quotes a passage from Deuteronomy 31:6 when he states:

"Keep your lives free from the love of money and be content with what you have, because God has said, 'Never will I leave you; / never will I forsake you.'" (13:5 NIV)

"Be strong and courageous. Do not be afraid or terrified because of them, for the LORD your God goes with you; he will never leave you nor forsake you."

Then Moses summoned Joshua and said to him in the presence of all Israel, "Be strong and courageous, for you must go with this people into the land that the LORD swore to their forefathers to give them, and you must divide it among them as their inheritance. The LORD himself goes before you and will be with you; he will never leave you nor forsake you. Do not be afraid; do not be discouraged." (Deuteronomy 31:6-8 NIV)

When James reflects back upon the purpose of the book of Job, he says:

"As you know, we consider blessed those who have persevered. You have heard of Job's perseverance and have seen what the Lord finally brought about. The Lord is full of compassion and mercy." (James 5:11 NIV)

Conclusion

Survivors may struggle with reconciling a view of God as good, faithful, powerful, and actively involved in the world in the face of their own adversity and suffering. C. S. Lewis confessed that when he turned to God for comfort at the death of his beloved wife, he instead found a door slammed in his face, "and a sound of bolting and double bolting on the inside" (1966, p. 9). In the aftermath, he readily admits that he found an understanding of God challenged in radical ways. In an open dialogue Lewis dares to expose the inner conflict of his soul: "Not that I am (I think) in much danger of ceasing to believe in God. The real danger is of coming to believe such dreadful things about Him. The conclusion I dread is not 'So there's no God after all,' but 'So this is what God's really like. Deceive yourself no longer'" (1996, pp. 9-10).

While in bondage in Babylon, the prophet Ezekiel wrote a simple phrase that speaks volumes to the effective caregiver, "I came to the exiles who lived at Tel Abib near the Kebar River. And there, where they were living, I sat among them for seven days—overwhelmed" (Ezekiel 3:15). Sent by God through a miracle journey to proclaim a strong message and overwhelmed by his call, he waited and sat where the exiles sat for seven days, feeling the pain of their affliction. Caregivers who minister to persons in traumatic events will frequently feel overwhelmed by the magnitude of pain and trauma of the situation. To sit where others sit before engaging in activities or ministry is a critical first element in being able to fulfill one's call to be with and help people in pain.

The word *sympathy* comes from the Greek word *sym*, "with," and *pathy*, which means "pain" or "sufferings." The word implies suffering with another or having the capacity of entering into the feelings or experience of the other. As authors, it is our desire that the church truly fulfill Jesus' desire that we become the active body of Christ filled with loving and compassionate caregivers who are willing to hear the painful wails of lament and to demonstrate the presence of an ever-faithful God. As a joyful and victorious people, we, the people of God, enter into the posttrauma journey with survivors, from initial impact to long-term transformation.

References

Andreasen, N. C. (1985). Posttraumatic stress disorder. In H. I. Kaplan and B. J. Sadock (Eds.), *Comprehensive textbook of psychiatry* (4th ed., pp. 918-24). Baltimore: Williams & Willkins.

Applebome. (2008, June 8). The day the traffic did not stop in Hartford. *The New York Times.*

Bachman, R. (1994, July 6). Violence and theft in the workplace. Crime Data Brief: National Crime Victimization survey.

Bolin, J. (1989). Natural disasters. In R. Gist & B. Lubin (Eds.). *Psychosocial aspects of disaster.* New York: John Wiley & Sons.

Bolin, J., and Bolton, P. (1986). *Race, religion, and ethnicity in disaster recovery.* Boulder: University of Colorado, Institute of Behavioral Science.

Breslau, N. (2001). The epidemiology of posttraumatic stress disorder: What is the extent of the problem? *Journal of Clinical Psychiatry 62* (Supplement 17), 16-22.

Breslau, N., Kessler, R., Chilcoat, H., Schulz, L., Davis, G., and Andreski, P. (1998). Trauma and posttraumatic stress disorder in the community. *Archives of General Psychiatry, 55,* 626-723.

Bryant, R. A., Guthrie, R. M., and Moulds, M. L. (2001). Hypnotizability in acute stress disorder. *American Journal of Psychiatry 158,* 600-604.

Bryant, R. A. and Harvey, A. G. (2000). *Acute stress disorder: A handbook of theory, assessment, and treatment.* Washington, DC: American Psychological Association.

Caplan, G. (1961). *An approach to community mental health.* New York: Grune and Stratton.

Caplan, G. (1964). *Principles of preventive psychiatry.* New York: Basic Books.

Creamer, M. and Manning, C. (1998). Acute stress disorder following an industrial accident. *Australian Psychologist 33,* 125-29.

Curbow, B., Legro, M. W., Baker, F., Wingard, J. R., and Sommerfield, M. R. (1993). Loss and recovery themes of long-term survivors of bone marrow transplant. *Journal of Psychosocial Oncology 10,* 1-20.

Davis, J. A. and Smith, T. W. (1995). General social surveys, 1972–1994. Chicago, IL: National Opinion Research Center [producer], 1994. Ann Arbor, MI: Inter-university Consortium for Political and Social Research [distributor].

Ellers, K. L. (2008). *Critical incident stress management: Emotional and spiritual care in disasters.* Ellicott City, MD: International Critical Incident Stress Foundation.

Ellers, K. L., Rikli, N., and Wright, H. N. (2006). *Critical incident stress management: Grief following trauma.* Ellicott City, MD: International Critical Incident Stress Foundation.

Everly, G. S., Jr. (1989). *A clinical guide to the treatment of the human stress response.* New York: Plenum Press.

Everly, G. S., Jr., Flannery, R. B., Jr., and Mitchell, J. T. (2000). Critical incident stress management: A review of literature. *Aggression and Violent Behavior: A Review Journal 5,* 23-40.

Everly, G. S., Jr., and Mitchell, J. T. (1999). Critical incident stress management (2nd ed.). Ellicott City, MD: Chevron Publishing Co.

Goleman, D. (1998). *Working with emotional intelligence*. New York: Bantam Books.

Halpern, H. A. (1973). Crisis theory: A definitional study. *Community Mental Health Journal 9*, 342-49.

Herman, J. L. (1997). *Trauma and recovery: The aftermath of violence from domestic abuse to political terror*. New York: Basic Books.

Hill, R. (1949). *Families under stress*. New York: Harper & Row.

Johnson, K. (1989). *Trauma in the lives of children: Crisis and stress management techniques for counselors and other professionals*. Alameda, CA: Hunter House Publishers.

Kardiner, A. and Spiegel, H. (1947). War, stress, and neurotic illness. New York: Hoeber.

Krug, E. G., Kresnow, M., Peddicord, J., Dahlberg, L., Powell, K., Crosby, A., and Annest, J. (1998). Suicide after natural disasters. *New England Journal of Medicine 338*, 373-78.

Lawrenz, M. and Green, D. R. (1995). *Life after grief: How to survive loss and trauma*. Grand Rapids, MI: Baker Books.

Lawrenz, M. and Green, D. R. (1995). *Overcoming grief and trauma: Strategic pastoral counseling resources*. Grand Rapids, MI: Baker Books.

Lehman, D. R., Davis, C. G., Delongis, A., Wortman, C. B., Bluck, S., Mandel, D. R., and Ellard, J. H. (1993). Positive and negative life changes following bereavement and their relations to adjustment. *Journal of Social and Clinical Psychology 12*, 90-112.

Leik, R. K., Leik, S. A., Ekker, K., and Gifford, G. A. (1982). *Under the threat of Mount St. Helens: A study of chronic family stress*. Minneapolis: University of Minnesota, Family Study Center.

Lewis, C. S. (1966). *A grief observed*. London: Faber and Faber.

Lindemann, E. (1944). Symptomatology and management of acute grief. *American Journal of Psychiatry 101*, 141-48.

McCubbin, H. I. and Patterson, J. (1983). The family stress process: The double ABCX model of adjustment and adaptation. In H. McCubbin and J. Patterson (Eds.). *Advances and developments in family stress theory and research* (pp. 7-37). Binghamton, NY: The Haworth Press.

McKenna, D. L. (1987). *The whisper of his grace: When we hurt and ask "Why?"* Waco, TX: Word Books.

Mileti, D. S., Drabek, T. E., and Haas, J. E. (1975). *Human systems in extreme environments: A sociological perspective.* Boulder: University of Colorado, Institute of Behavioral Science.

Mitchell, J. T. (2006). *Critical incident stress management (CISM): Group crisis intervention.* Ellicott City, MD: International Critical Incident Stress Foundation.

O'Connor, A. P., Wicker, C. A., and Germino, B. B. (1990). Understanding the cancer patient's search for meaning. *Cancer Nursing 13*, 167-75.

Patterson, J. and Garwick, A. (1994). Levels of meaning in family stress theory. *Family Process 33* (3), 287-304.

Powlison, D. (2006). God's grace and your sufferings in Piper, John and Taylor, John, *Suffering and the sovereignty of God.* Wheaton, IL: Crossway Books.

Quarantelli, E. L. (1985). Social support systems: Some behavioral patterns in the context of mass evacuation activities. In B. Sowder (Ed.). *Disasters and mental health: Selected contemporary perspectives* (DHHS Publication No. ADM85-1421, pp. 122-36). Washington, DC: U.S. Government Printing Office.

Raphael, B. (1986). *When disaster strikes.* New York: Basic Books.

Reed, P. (1987). Spirituality and well-being in terminal hospitalized adults. *Research in Nursing and Health 10,* 355-44.

Schwartzberg, S. S. and Janoff-Bulman, R. (1991). Grief and the search for meaning: Exploring the assumptive worlds of bereaved college students. *Journal of Social and Clinical Psychology 10,* 270-88.

Selye, H. (1976). *The stress of life.* New York: McGraw Hill Book Co.

Sherman, S. (1994, August 22). Leaders learn to heed the voice within. *Fortune.*

Silber, T. J. and Reilly, M. (1985). Spiritual and religious concerns of the hospitalized adolescent. *Adolescence 20,* 217-24.

Slaikeu, K. A. (1990). *Crisis intervention.* Boston: Allyn and Bacon.

About the Authors

Kevin L. Ellers, DMin

Kevin is the Territorial Disaster Services Coordinator for The Salvation Army in the U.S.A. Central Territory. He is also president of the Institute for Compassionate Care, which is dedicated to education, training, and direct care. He is a chaplain with the Illinois Fraternal Order of Police, serves as faculty for the International Critical Incident Stress Foundation, and is a member of the American Association of Christian Counselors Crisis Response Training Team. He has extensive training and experience in crisis response, disasters, chaplaincy, pastoral ministries, marriage and family therapy, and social services, and as an author and speaker teaches broadly in these related topics.

Jennifer Cisney, MA, CRT

Jennifer Cisney is the Team Coordinator for the National Crisis Response Team of the American Association of Christian Counselors (AACC). She also is Director of AACC's Christian Crisis Response Training Program. She led AACC's response in New York City following 9/11 and functions as coordinator for all of AACC's responses to local and national disasters. She is a member of AACC's National Crisis Training Team.

CPSIA information can be obtained at www.ICGtesting.com
Printed in the USA
LVOW01s0904180114

369981LV00018B/1498/P